COACH UP

50 RULES

FOR BUILDING COMMITTED, CONFIDENT, AND MOTIVATED ATHLETES AND TEAMS

Greg A. Shelley, Ph.D.
Foreword by Jeff Janssen

This publication is designed to provide accurate and authoritative information in regard to the subject matter covered. It is sold with the understanding that the publisher is not engaged in rendering legal, accounting, or other professional services. If legal advice or other expert assistance is required, the services of a competent professional person should be sought.

Published by:
Rise Above Performance Publications
3291 Jacksonville Road
Trumansburg, NY 14886
Phone: 607-220-3760
Fax: 607-387-8611
Email: gshelley@ithaca.edu
Website : www.riseaboveconsult.com

Printed by:
MomentumMedia
20 Eastlake Road
Ithaca, NY 14850
Website : www.momentummedia.com

ISBN 978-0-9835831-6-5
Published in the United States of America

FOREWORD

I am excited and honored to write the foreword for *Coach Up*! Coaching is a calling that is both noble and challenging: Noble in that you get the awesome opportunity to inspire and impact human beings as athletes and people. Challenging in that each athlete is unique, responding quite differently to your communication, motivation, leadership, etc. Thus, coaching truly is an art form that benefits from ongoing reflection, learning, and application.

I love a lot of things about *Coach Up* but the two things I appreciate the most are the book's practicality and insightfulness. I love the fact that the lessons are presented in bite-sized chunks that every busy coach can quickly read, digest, and apply in their hectic schedules. Whether you are an assistant coach just starting out or a veteran coach who is at the top of your profession, this gem of a book is something every coach can turn to when looking for immediate ideas and actionable advice.

While some of you will likely read this book from cover to cover, others might simply focus on and implement one of the key lessons to improve yourself, your staff, and team virtually every week of the year. Athletic Directors will especially love this resource because it gives them a tremendous professional development tool for their coaches throughout the course of a year.

Coach Up is also highly insightful. It reminds us all about the important intangibles that are so critical to success both on and off the playing fields. The little things like confidence, chemistry, commitment, and competitiveness are often the BIG things that matter most. Too many times we take the intangibles for granted until they come back to bite us. Greg puts these critical intangibles on the forefront of our minds and gives us proven tips to develop and address them within our daily lives. *Coach Up* helps you ask the right questions that get to the heart of the matter - and provides you with proven strategies to solve your toughest coaching challenges.

Having known Greg as a trusted friend and valued colleague over many years, he is the perfect person to write this book. He has decades of experience working with athletes and coaches from the youth to the professional levels. He has experienced the sports world from all angles: successfully playing the roles of athlete, coach, sports parent, consultant, Leadership Academy facilitator, and sport psychology professor. Thus, he has been in the locker rooms, dugouts, huddles, and late night coaches meetings for epic wins and crushing defeats; so he knows what works, and just as importantly, how to avoid what doesn't work.

Not only has Greg made a meaningful career out of helping others learn how to succeed and handle setbacks, he models what he writes in his relationships as a consultant, professor, father, husband, and friend. His life is a testament to the effectiveness of these principles.

You will most certainly be a better coach and all-around leader by reading and applying just a small fraction of all the great ideas presented in *Coach Up*. More importantly, you will find yourself becoming a better parent, spouse, friend, and overall person as the result of reading it. Enjoy this fantastic book and keep Coaching Up!

Jeff Janssen, Janssen Sports Leadership Center
Author of *The Team Captain's Leadership Manual*
and The Commitment Continuum™ System

DEDICATION

To Stacy: My better half, best friend, and *full-time* assistant coach. **I love you**.

To Anna: **I . . . love . . . you . . . Anna . . . always.**

To Jake: **Captain . . . I love ya'.**

It's a privilege to be called *family*. I have been blessed beyond words. Thank you for putting up with my coaching blunders as I forever try to "*coach up*" the rules on the following pages. Thanks to each of you for your ongoing patience as I continue to work on becoming a better husband, dad, and *coach*.

You're the BEST!

ACKNOWLEDGMENTS

Success is rarely achieved alone. Coaches are successful because they are organized, prepared, work hard, *and* because they have committed and dedicated coaching staffs and players. In the same way, my successes have been, and continue to be tied to a "team" of talented, devoted, and loyal colleagues, clients, friends, and family. My insights and experiences are a result of the many coaches, athletes, teams, administrators, colleagues, students, and family members that have influenced my writings, teachings, and consulting. To all, I am forever grateful. It is a pleasure to acknowledge some of my team here.

First, thank you to countless coaches, athletes, and administrators I have had the privilege to work with over the past 24 years. I especially want to thank the hundreds of coaches and athletes at Binghamton, Carnegie Mellon, Colgate, Cornell, Delaware, Fordham, Georgetown, Iowa, Lafayette, Syracuse, Utah, and Wake Forest. I also want to thank the coaches, athletes, and administrators at Hobart and William Smith College and Ithaca College. Year after year you have allowed me into your sporting worlds and taught me more than you will ever know. Thank you for your trust and willingness to work with me.

Thank you to Jeff Janssen for your continuous sharing of knowledge, wisdom, and experiences. You have trusted me to come along side you (and your team) to help develop and grow the best sports leadership academies available. Thank you for including me and always challenging me to improve and grow, personally and professionally. You are a trusted colleague and friend.

Thank you to Bobby Dughi and Raymond Prior. You regularly challenge me in how I develop, refine, and deliver sport consulting services. Your vision and enthusiasm for success is refreshing and encouraging. Thank you for including me on your team too. And thanks for *always* making me laugh. You will forever be "family" and your friendships priceless.

Thank you to Mark Goldberg and the entire *MomentumMedia* team for accepting this project and walking me through the editing and printing process. I especially want to thank Eleanor, Maria, Neal, Sharon, Pennie, and Trish, for all your work, insights, creativity, and leadership. This book would not have gone to print without your combined efforts and teamwork. Thank you for your knowledge and patience.

Most of all, I want to thank my family. Anna and Jake, thank you for putting up with a dad that sometimes fails to follow the rules he writes about. Thank you for your patience, love, and acceptance, especially on the days that I don't deserve it. **Anna**, I admire your competitive spirit and your desire to "play up" . . . outside your "comfort zone." You inspire me to work hard and do "extra" every day! Your drive, persistence, and passion will take you far in life. Keep raising the bar and expecting more from yourself than others expect from you. Lead by example and always be the hardest worker on your team. It is a mark of a true champion. **Jake**, you constantly remind me about the importance of a positive attitude. Your personality is refreshing and your optimism is contagious! You inspire me to remain positive, regardless of the situation or outcome and you model for me what it is to be a great team player and trusted teammate. Your attitude will be the foundation of many great teams in your life. Dare to set the standard, even when it is not what everyone else is doing. Keep leading from your heart, doing the right thing, and genuinely caring for your teammates and friends. To both of you . . . keep thinking, acting, and leading like champions. You are both winners. I thank God for you and I look forward to watching you grow and mature. I love you both and I am truly blessed and honored to be called your dad.

And **Stacy**, I cannot do what I do without you. Thank you for allowing me time to teach, consult, and write. When I arrive home from work or travel, you *always* seem to have our "house in order." You are a fantastic mom and wife. You are the "glue" that keeps this family running smoothly and with love. Thank you for taking care of us and for keeping our team together! Please keep "*coaching up.*" I need you much more than you think . . . and much more than I tell you. A simple "thank you" is not enough . . . but with all my heart, "Thank you!" You are the captain of this team we call family. I love you.

TABLE OF CONTENTS

PART IV:
The Rules of Leadership

PART V:
The Rules of Communication

PART VI:
The Rules of Mental Toughness

INTRODUCTION

Welcome to ***Coach Up: 50 rules for building committed, confident, and motivated athletes and teams***. Whether a seasoned head coach of 25 years or a new assistant coach just starting out, this book contains practical "hands on" rules for developing high performing athletes and winning teams. Some of the following rules are simple and easy to implement into your daily coaching routines. Some you already know and some, for whatever reason, you may ignore. Of course, some rules are difficult to carry out and will demand additional thought and planning before adding to your already established coaching practices. There are no gimmicks, shortcuts, or tricks to becoming a great coach. The best coaches have a clear vision, relentlessly prepare, wholeheartedly commit, unselfishly lead, and persistently follow-through with what they start.

Becoming a better coach always starts with self reflection. To improve your coaching, you will have to improve *you*. Better coaching starts by adhering to the rules outlined in the following pages. They are direct, concise, and proven effective. In short, they work and they are your guide to becoming a better coach.

Each rule is its own chapter . . . 50 rules and 50 short chapters. Each chapter is complete with detailed coaching information, coaching challenges, and strategies for improvement. The phrase ***"coach up"*** is used throughout the book. Each chapter includes ***"COACH UP Strategies"*** containing practical, "how-to" take-home points for immediate coaching application. This book is about coach improvement . . . and challenging you to be a better coach. It's about enhancing motivation, building stronger teams, developing better leaders, establishing more effective communication, and improving athlete mental toughness and confidence. This book is about coaching the "intangibles." It's about promoting, encouraging, empowering, teaching, and mentoring your athletes. It's about doing the "little things" that produce winners and winning teams.

The book is divided into six parts. ***Part I*** presents a foundational set of coaching rules for developing greater preparation, commitment, attitude, trust, and passion. ***Part II*** outlines strategies for developing athlete motivation, inspiring commitment, and building strong coach-athlete relationships. ***Part III*** promotes ways for building efficient and productive teams and team climates. ***Part IV*** highlights a process for developing and mentoring strong leaders and captains. ***Part V*** contains rules for establishing effective coach-athlete and coach-coach communication. And ***Part VI*** details how to "coach up" confident, composed, resilient, and mentally tough athletes. Each section has its own set of rules. Although presented in a logical order with some rules building upon a previous rule, the content of each rule is more important than the order in which it is presented. So, start with reading Rule 1 or pick the section that is most relevant to your coaching needs right now. I hope you are challenged, encouraged, and inspired as you go. Read and re-read the rules as needed. Grow, improve, and expand your coaching. Remember, great coaching starts with your willingness to make a change. Go ahead ***"coach up"*** . . . and enjoy the rewards of better coaching. You'll be well on your way to building more committed, confident, and motivated athletes and teams.

The Rules of Coaching

C.O.A.C.H. U.P.

"If you want to build an atmosphere in which everybody pulls together to win, then you, as a leader have to recognize that it all starts with you. It starts with your attitude, your commitment, your caring, your passion for excellence, your dedication to winning. It starts with the example you set."
— **Pat Williams**

It is an honor to be called "coach" . . . and a privilege to have the opportunity to ***"coach up"*** athletes and teams each day. As the coach, you wear many hats. On any day you might be a coach, mentor, teacher, counselor, motivator, conflict manager, communication specialist, physiologist, sport psychologist, strength and conditioning expert, nutritionist, administrator, sports director, team-builder, recruiter, or team leader. It is an honor . . . but it is also a challenge.

> Coaching is about knowing what to coach, how and when to coach, and being clear with your reasons for why you are coaching.

Having good coaching intentions is a good start but it's not enough. No doubt, you need specific sport knowledge and age appropriate coaching skills unique to your sport, players, and team goals. However, that too is not enough. You need more. You need to teach your athletes how to respond to mistakes and losses, how to play with passion, change attitudes, play together and trust one another, communicate, lead, develop confidence and mental toughness, deal with pressure, prepare better, and seek out opportunities to grow, refine skills, and mature as an athlete and a person. Coaching is about knowing what to coach, how and when to coach, and being clear with your reasons for why you are coaching.

Successful coaching is also about winning. For some of you, your job is dependent upon wins and losses. For many, winning is not the final outcome that decides your future. Of course, everyone likes to win and, deep down, everyone wants to win. Even for those few that say winning or losing doesn't matter, it usually does. Winning is more fun than losing . . . it's just the way it is. So, coach to win! Challenge your athletes to compete, play with passion, and pursue victory each and every day. You should never have to apologize for *playing to win*. Just be sure that your pursuit of victory is fair, ethical, within the rules and guidelines established, and in line with the age-appropriate practices of your organization, league, school, conference, or institution. Yes, it's an honor to be called coach. Go ahead, **Coach up** your athletes to be the best they can be . . . today, this season, and for years to come.

COACH UP Strategies

C = Competence. Effective coaching is about knowing the X's and O's, monitoring offensive and defensive schemes, making practice and competition adjustments, understanding your opponents' tendencies, knowing your own strengths and weaknesses, and teaching appropriate sport skills based on the age and skill level of your athletes. Great coaching entails managing the practice and competitive environments as well as managing player emotions, individual "psyches," team trust, group cohesion, leadership, and responses to mistakes and setbacks. A competent coach is well versed in the physical, emotional, psychological, and social aspects of coaching. Without coaching competence, what follows really doesn't matter.

O = Opportunity. The best coaches look for every opportunity to get better. They look for new drills, new coaching strategies, and new advances in technology, equipment, and ways of communicating. A win is an opportunity to encourage team members. A loss is an opportunity to learn, refine, and get better. A new book is an opportunity to learn a new perspective. Talking with coaching colleagues, consultants, and fellow staff members is an opportunity to be informed of "new ways" *and* "better ways" of doing things. And finally, an honest review of year-end coach evaluations is an opportunity to be honest about what *is* working and what *is not* working, as well as an opportunity to change and advance your coaching effectiveness. The best coaches see growth opportunities everywhere they look.

> The best coaches look for every opportunity to get better.

A = Attitude. Attitude is everything (see Rule 2). The most influential coaches arrive to work each day with a "can do" attitude and look to challenge and encourage positive individual and team growth. These coaches bring their best coaching every day . . . and look to build up and esteem their athletes with positive words and actions. Attitude is about what you say, what you do, and the facial expressions and body language that follow. Your attitude is likely the most important factor impacting your team climate . . . and your attitude will make or break your daily practices and competitions. Positive attitude entails focusing on what you have, as opposed to what you don't have. The right attitude is void of complaining and whining and is centered on "getting things done."

C = Commitment, Composure, and Consistency. Committed coaches just do more than everybody else. They are *committed* to getting better themselves, gaining a competitive edge, and doing "extra" (above and beyond what is expected and completed by other coaches). Most of all, they are committed to their athletes, building strong relationships, and providing opportunities for success. In short, they are committed to being the best coach possible. The best coaches also seem to be the most *composed*. When other coaches lose control of their emotions, the composed coach keeps coaching. When some coaches become consumed by bad calls, argue with officials, and focus on "bad plays" . . . the composed coach keeps a calm demeanor and stays focused on what is relevant. And finally, the best coaches do all these things *consistently*. Anybody can have a good coaching day. However, the best coaches make a habit of good coaching. They consistently coach at a high level . . . day in and day out. They come to expect great coaching from themselves and their staff. They are consistent in their thoughts, actions, and outcomes. Great coaches demand great coaching every day.

H = Humility. A humble coach "knows what they don't know." They know they have more to learn and they know they can get better. They know that another book, conversation, coaching clinic, game film, or talk with a consultant might yield a better way of coaching. At the very least it might produce a new and better way of thinking. The humble coach knows that if they look hard enough . . . they can find a way to improve. They know there are more experienced coaches to learn from and better coaching practices to adopt. Humble coaches never stop learning and improving. They also give credit (in good times) and take the blame (in bad times). Humility is a mark of a great coach.

U = Unconditional Support and Encouragement. Support and encouragement are great motivators. The best coaches have a "knack" for offering an encouraging word to a struggling athlete . . . and doing so at just the right time. They also have a way of showing their unconditional support when the athlete needs it most. The term "unconditional" means that the support or encouragement is not dependent upon getting the desired outcome. The best coaches understand this and support and encourage their athletes through mistakes, slumps, relational struggles, academic shortcomings, and personal failures. Holding the athlete accountable is still a priority but unconditional support and encouragement is about giving "second chances" and mentoring players through "tough-times." Unconditional support is about not giving up on someone when everyone else has . . . and encouraging them to persevere and "stay the course." The best coaches regularly support and encourage their athletes and staff . . . especially when others don't.

> Humble coaches never stop learning and improving.

P = Preparation and Passion. Some coaches prepare more . . . and some coaches prepare smarter. Whatever the situation, the best coaches are *prepared*. They have watched the film, strategized, developed practice and competition plans, communicated clear expectations to their staff and players, conducted organized practice sessions, assigned the proper leadership, and followed-up as needed. The prepared coach is ready to go and is rarely surprised or "caught off guard." In addition, the best coaches have great *passion*. They talk and act with passion and there is never a question concerning their "love of coaching." They are enthusiastic, excited, and opportunistic about what is to come. They are genuinely excited to see what the next practice brings and how the team will grow, develop, and perform. They love the game and they love coaching . . . and it shows.

"The answer to three questions will determine your success or failure. One, can people trust me to do my best? Two, am I committed to the task at hand? Three, do I care about other people and show it? If the answer to all three questions is yes, there is no way you can fail."

- Lou Holtz

Attitude is everything

"The greatest discovery of any generation is that a human being can alter his life by altering his attitude."

- William James

Let me get right to the point: Your coaching attitude is far more important than any of your coaching duties. What you are asked to do is *not* as important as how (and with what attitude) you do it. Do not underestimate your "coaching attitude" because it will directly influence the way your athletes think and feel. In simple terms, your attitude will make or break your team. There is no middle of the road with attitude. Your attitude is either influencing your athletes in a positive *or* negative way. Your attitude is pushing your team down or it's pulling your team up.

The best thing about attitude is that you can change it in an instance. To change, however, means you must choose to be "out with the old and in with the new." You will have to commit to getting rid of the old (bad) attitude and adopting a new (good) attitude. Of course, the new attitude must be maintained and you must be consistent from moment to moment, situation to situation, and day to day. Successful coaches choose the right attitude and maintain it. They are consistent in adopting the right attitude, consistent in how they positively influence individual athletes, and consistent in creating a positive team climate. The goal is to create a team climate that allows for the best chance of success (see Rule 26). Your attitude is contagious . . . make sure it's positive.

COACH UP Strategies

1. Take the 30 day attitude challenge. The challenge is to change your attitude for 30 days (it takes about 30 days to create a habit). Be honest here. Make note of specific situations in which you struggle keeping a good attitude . . . or those individuals with whom you find it difficult to maintain a good attitude. In these situations and around these individuals, your challenge becomes "pulling" your bad attitude and "planting" a good attitude. There is no magical formula . . . you simply choose to take the *30 day challenge* in which you adopt and "live out" your new coach attitude. Take the challenge and make the change. Your athletes and staff *will* notice!

2. Go beyond the unexpected. It's an obvious statement but . . . things just don't always go as planned. Prepare for the unexpected. Setbacks, mistakes, and failures are inevitable. While many coaches respond to the unexpected with a questionable attitude, your response should be to *go beyond* the unexpected and remain positive and focused on what is yet to be accomplished. This means you remain focused on the goal, how the goal can be accomplished, and the appropriate attitude needed to achieve it. The right attitude must be maintained throughout the entire practice, day, or week (i.e., drill, practice, game, or tournament). Don't let your attitude stop your team from attaining the expected goal.

3. Coach with optimism. One of the most important things you can do is remain optimistic and hopeful. Athletes want to be around coaches who are optimistic, enthusiastic, hopeful, and confident. Talk in terms of what your team *will* accomplish rather than what they *should* accomplish. Attitudes surrounding "what will be achieved" are very different than those surrounding "what *should* be achieved." Your optimism will have a direct impact on your players' response to mistakes, confidence, focus, and overall commitment. An optimistic attitude spreads quickly. Stay focused on what *will* be accomplished and be that coach who instills hope and optimism every day.

> An optimistic attitude spreads quickly.

"There's only one thing more contagious than a good attitude – and that's a bad attitude."

- John Maxwell

You move in the direction of what you think

"Something good is about to happen."

- Pete Carroll

Every action begins with a thought. For most people, their first thoughts tend to be negative and focused on weaknesses rather than strengths, on what could go wrong rather than what will go right, or on past failures rather than future successes. Positive thinking is not easy. In fact, moving forward with consistent positive thoughts may be one of the most difficult things you do over the course of a day or week. It seems normal to first think about the negative things that could go wrong or have already gone wrong. Yet, successful coaches think different. They overcome negative thinking patterns by turning unproductive, pessimistic thoughts into productive, positive thoughts. The best coaches focus on and implement *"forward thinking"* . . . thinking that is geared toward positive, future performance outcomes.

> The best coaches focus on and implement *"forward thinking"* . . . thinking that is geared toward positive, future performance outcomes.

It's not easy to change your thinking . . . but it is necessary for long-term coaching success. *What you think about is what you move toward.* If you think about success you move in the direction of success. If you think about your coaching strengths, you move in the direction of using and focusing on your strengths. When you practice *positive forward thinking*, your coaching will improve and your staff, athletes, and team will benefit.

COACH UP Strategies

1. Think "big." This means clarifying and talking about your team vision and promoting teamwork in such a way that your athletes see the "bigger-picture." It's very important that your athletes understand how their individual roles and responsibilities impact the team and reaching team goals. Thinking big can keep you and your team focused, striving for the ultimate goal, and ready to seize the moment at just the right time.

2. Think "strengths." This means maintaining a "strength focus." You should spend the majority of your time using your gifts, talents, and best coaching attributes. If possible, delegate your weaker skills to another coach or someone else who can complete the skill as well as, or better than, you. Take time to focus your thinking on what needs to be done now and what *you* are best at doing. In the long run, you will be more productive and efficient because you consistently use your best coaching skills. Be sure to approach each day with a strength focus.

3. Think "reflection." This means slowing down (even stopping at times), revisiting what you have heard or observed, and then putting your new thoughts into an action plan. Slowing down and reflecting on what has already taken place is often difficult. There never seems to be enough time to stop and assess. However, it is extremely important to set aside time to reflect on your own coaching philosophy, coach leadership, the practice environment that you are attempting to create each day, or whatever else might need some attention. A little "reflection" might be exactly what your team needs in order to experience a positive change and continue to move forward.

4. Think "new and better." This means taking what you have learned and experienced in the past and turning these experiences into something even better. Be creative with new coaching ideas and methods, but also know your ideas do not have to be original. You can model a new way of coaching, a new offense, or a revamped practice plan from another coach or program. In the end, the goal is to learn more, challenge the status quo, and better your program. Your creativity might well be your most valuable coaching resource. Athletes typically respond well to coaches that present new and novel ways (options) for getting better.

5. Think "staff." This means collaborating, thinking, and regularly talking with the rest of your coaching staff. Two minds really *are* better than one! And it makes perfect sense that when you and your staff combine your thoughts . . . you come up with new (and better) ideas. This is also true when you have younger staff members that can provide "new perspectives" and new ways for doing things. Collaborating with your staff can help you overcome a lack of vision, knowledge, experience, as well as unforeseen obstacles that surface throughout the season. Whatever you do, you will likely do it better with the help of others on your staff.

"Two are better than one, because they have a good return on their work: If one falls down, his friend can help him up. But pity the man who falls and has no one to help him up."
- Ecclesiastes 4:9-10 (NIV)

People before coaching

"The key to developing people is to catch them doing something right."

- Ken Blanchard and Spencer Johnson

Good coaching starts with positive influence. Influence comes in the form of the words you speak, the look on your face, the behaviors you model, the effort and intensity you display, and your responses to the situations (good *and* bad) you face. You are always influencing someone. Your athletes "look to you" to influence them toward success! Although they don't ask, your athletes want you to be a model for them, motivate them in difficult times, refocus them when faced with obstacles and mistakes, and hold them accountable to a higher standard of play. In short, they want your support, encouragement, and consistent challenges to improve. That's what coaches do . . . they move their athletes toward improvement. Without your positive influence, your team *will* fall short in reaching its potential. Positive influence usually leads to positive outcomes. Influence starts and ends with the relationships you form with others. You must effectively (and consistently) interact with your athletes, other coaches, administrators, and parents. No doubt, your ability to relate to and positively interact with others will directly impact your long-term coaching effectiveness. With that said, your athletes will "buy in" to you (the person) first, before they embrace what you ask them to do. When they can relate to you, they will listen to you. When they know you care, they will do what you ask. Remember, people *before* coaching.

COACH UP Strategies

1. Your athletes want authentic relationships. Go out of your way to be honest, genuine, and "real." Your athletes need to know they can come to you at any time and trust you to have their best interests at heart. Whatever the situation, they must know that they can count on you to be authentic (no pretense or uncertainty). Most athletes want authentic coaches who are approachable, dependable, fair, and honest.

2. Your athletes want a leader to follow. Your athletes are looking for a leader, so make sure that leader is you. Athletes need to know they can depend on you to lead them, set the tone for what is to come, and help them through whatever obstacles that might surface in the future. They want a strong, trusted leader to follow in good *and* bad times.

3. Your athletes are struggling with something. Be sure to encourage and empower your athletes whenever possible. Athletes need to hear something positive in the midst of a bad day of classes, a broken dating relationship, roommate problems, difficult family issues, bad performances, or an on-going losing streak. Engage and esteem your athletes. Make your athlete's day . . . say something nice!

4. Your athletes need help in responding to mistakes. In the face of mistakes and failures, be sure to help your athletes refocus on their strengths, control their emotions, and focus on relevant cues to ensure future success (for more on focusing and refocusing athletes, see Rule 47). Most athletes are overly critical in the face of failure and need your help refocusing on *what to do next* rather than the mistake just made or what has already been completed. The mistake is not the focus . . . appropriately responding to the mistake is. Help your athletes move past their mistakes and failings. Do not underestimate your help here . . . many athletes need assistance in appropriately responding to their mistakes.

> The mistake is not the focus . . . appropriately responding to the mistake is.

"It's about the journey- -mine and yours- -and the lives we can touch, the legacy we can leave, and the world we can change for the better."

- Tony Dungy

Be trustworthy

"To be trusted is a greater compliment than being loved."

-George MacDonald

Do your athletes trust you? Does your staff trust you? At the end of the day, are you trustworthy? Each day the level of trust on your team is getting better (increasing) or getting worse (decreasing). What you say, how you say it, what you do, and when you do it are all factors influencing whether or not your athletes and staff trust you. Your words and actions impact every team meeting, practice, and competition. Trust defines all great teams, and similarly, defines your team. As a coach, you play a critical role in defining and developing your "team trust." In short, team trust is closely tied to your coach leadership. You are regularly called on for your input, direction, and answers (e.g., conflicts to be resolved, decisions to be made, intensity and effort to be defined, attitude redefined, and skills to be corrected). You are trustworthy when you *consistently* lead by example, encourage your athletes toward success, and hold players accountable to an agreed upon standard of excellence. How much your athletes trust you will also impact how much they are willing to trust one another. In the end, coach-athlete trust directly impacts the team climate, how teammates work together, and how they hold one another accountable.

Trust is often talked about but rarely achieved . . . and building trust is difficult and time consuming. What takes years to build can be destroyed in minutes. No doubt, trust can be fragile and fleeting. So . . . devote considerable time to building *and* maintaining long-lasting, trustworthy relationships.

COACH UP Strategies

1. Say it, mean it, and do it. Keep your word. If you promise something, then keep your promise. If it's a phone call, text, or email you promised, follow through. If you said you would stop by and say hello, do so. If you told an athlete that you would find an answer to a question, find the answer and report back to him or her promptly. When you do not follow through, those around you begin to question (and do so quickly) whether or not you can be trusted.

2. Speak the truth and nothing but the truth. The truth always rises to the top. The truth is trustworthy. If you speak the truth . . . you *are* trustworthy. If you are not speaking the truth, gossiping, or "talking behind another's back" - you cannot be trusted. It's really that simple. You can "fake" the truth for a short time but at some point you will be faced with speaking the truth. You may not be the most liked person when you speak the truth but, in time, you will be trusted and respected. Others will always know where you stand and they will learn to count on you for the truth, whatever the occasion.

3. Prepare more than everyone expects. There is no substitute for preparation. You must *always* know what you are doing. Great preparation and planning directly impact your coach credibility. Being credible gives your athletes and fellow coaches (and anyone else you work with) a reason to trust you. Trust develops when you consistently show your commitment to others by way of hard work, clear goals, action plans, and results. Your athletes will quickly learn to trust your preparation and commitment, knowing that you have provided them, at the very least, a chance to succeed. Prepare more. Work hard. No excuses!

> There is no substitute for preparation.

"Few things can help an individual more than to place responsibility on him, and to let him know that you trust him."

-Booker T. Washington

Dare to be different

"Change before you have to."

- Jack Welch

t's easy to become complacent and accept that "things are what they are." For many athletes, what is about to happen today is simply an extension of what happened yesterday. The drills performed today are the same drills that were performed yesterday (and will be performed tomorrow). What many athletes are asked to do is simply repeat what they have already performed many times in previous practices. Without question, this "repetition" is good! In fact, repetition is often the cornerstone for refining and perfecting many sport skills. But to get better, some athletes must *"tweak"* what they expect, say, do, and how they act and respond. They may need to *tweak* their goals, their attitude toward practice, their mental training strategies, their nutritional habits, or their commitment to off-season training. For many athletes, a simple "tweak" is all that is needed. However, some athletes (and teams) need more. They need some form of a *"makeover."* A makeover is about creating and doing something entirely new and different (for a special occasion, game, tournament, or season). It's about thinking something new, preparing something new, and doing something new. An athlete makeover might include developing new goals and goal achievement strategies, implementing a new pre-season mental training program, or adopting a new plan for off-season conditioning. A coaching makeover might entail a new offense or defense, a new coaching strategy, a new way to manage athletes, a new way of communicating, a new reward structure, or a new way for holding athletes accountable. In the end, some things need tweaked and some things need a makeover. Go ahead, *dare to be different . . .* look to tweak *and* makeover!

COACH UP Strategies

> To seize the moment means to be in the moment.

1. Seize the moment. Learn from the past but *coach in the moment.* Coaching in the moment means moving past what *has* happened and focusing on what *is* happening. It's about helping your athletes get past *what was . . .* and focus on *what is.* To seize the moment means to be in the moment. Let the last play, series, call, game, or tournament . . . be done. *Get on with getting on.* Seize the present moment so that your athletes can also seize the moment. Set the example and focus your athletes (and your entire team) on what is here and now.

2. Shape the moment. Once you have seized the moment . . . you are ready to shape it. Shaping the moment is about *demanding* the right attitude, focus, communication, response to mistakes, and commitment to what you are asking . . . **RIGHT NOW!** Shaping the moment is about controlling emotions, remaining patient, and trusting your coaching strategies and game plans. It's about keeping your athletes thinking about, talking about, and doing what is most important right now. Shaping the moment is about shaping the environment in such a way that everyone's energy is directed toward accomplishing the task at hand. There is no wasted energy or time spent complaining or whining. Shaping the moment is about the entire team working together in a controlled and confident manner.

> Shaping the moment is about shaping the environment in such a way that everyone's energy is directed toward accomplishing the task at hand.

3. Stamp the moment. Make the moment yours. Own the moment! If what you are doing is working, finish the job. If things need *"tweaked,"* make the needed changes, and then finish the job. If something is in need of a *"makeover,"* then do it for the next play, series, quarter, or half (or the next game or meet) . . . but whatever you do, finish the job. Stamp the moment as your moment (and your team's moment). Determine how you want others to label you and your team . . . then make it happen. Will you be known for how you coach in the clutch? Will you be known as a coach who makes good decisions? Will you be known as a coach who is cool, calm, and in control? How about your team? Will your team play with unity? Will it be known as a mentally tough team? Will it be known as a physically demanding team that plays hard to the end? Whatever the stamp, decide what you want to be known for and demand it from yourself and your athletes. Seize the moment, shape the moment . . . then stamp the moment!

"The important thing is this: to be ready at any moment to sacrifice what you are for what you could become."

- Charles Dickens

Learn from other coaches' mistakes

"Smart people learn from their mistakes. But the real sharp ones learn from the mistakes of others."

- Brandon Mull

t's not *if* you will make mistakes . . . you will. In the end, it's about how you respond to the mistakes you do make. Of course, the fewer mistakes you make . . . the better. To make fewer mistakes, you must learn from your previous mistakes. In addition, *you must learn from others' mistakes.* That's right . . . it's important to examine your coaching colleagues, assess their mistakes, and do

> Examining other coaches' mistakes *now* can save you from making the same mistakes *later.*

everything you can to steer clear of making the same mistakes. This means you understand the mistakes made by other coaches and ask what went wrong, how and why the mistakes happened, and whether or not similar mistakes could happen in your program or organization. Examining other coaches' mistakes *now* can save you from making the same mistakes *later*.

COACH UP Strategies

1. Find out what went wrong. When another coach is "guilty of wrongdoings," find out what went wrong. Whether the mistake was a result of a coaching blunder, a recruiting violation, a character flaw, or any other inappropriate action or reaction by a coach . . . learn the details and get the full story. While unfortunate for that coach, you might as well learn from his or her mistake. When assessing what went wrong, find out exactly how and why the mistake happened. What were the circumstances surrounding the mistake? How and why did the media respond as they did? Was the coaching staff truthful? Were the mistakes discussed and addressed in a timely manner? Why did events unfold as they did? Why did coaches respond as they did? How did the administration respond? In short, how and why did the mistake happen? Be sure to answer as many how and why questions as possible. The more you know now . . . the more you (and your staff) can avoid later.

2. Ask yourself if it could happen in your program. Be honest here. Have you ever made the same mistake? Have you made the same comments, reacted the same way, or written the same words (but not found yourself in the same mess)? If "yes," count your blessings! If "no," then prepare as you have and continue your current ways of thinking, reacting, or responding. Just be honest. Is it possible to make a similar mistake in the future? Learn from your coaching colleagues! It's not fun watching your colleagues suffer the consequences of their mistakes. However, it *will* be worse if you too find yourself suffering similar consequences because you did not learn from their mistakes.

3. Make the needed changes. Finally, make all needed changes. If anger needs to be controlled, find a way to control it. If critical coaching needs to stop, do what is needed to implement more positive coaching practices. If recruiting practices need to be altered, get on it. If a bad (wrong) decision was made today, make the right one tomorrow. If you have "lost control" of any part of your program, then prioritize getting that part of your program under control. Do what needs to be done and do it now! Make these changes a priority. Be proactive in your coaching and take every opportunity to learn from your own mistakes, as well as others' mistakes. Minimize your mistakes so that you can maximize your coaching.

"Mistakes are the growing pains of wisdom."

- William Jordan

Stop the "ruckus"

"Don't complain; just work harder."

- Randy Pausch

Remember, you move in the direction of what you think (see Rule 3). With that in mind . . . *"Just Stop!"* Stop complaining, blaming, arguing, and pointing fingers. When you do these things, you create *"ruckus."* Ruckus serves no good purpose and will only distract you from your goal of better coaching. Complaining about poor playing conditions, blaming referees and umpires for bad calls, or pointing

> In simple terms, ruckus responses are distracting.

fingers at specific mistakes made will not move you or your team toward more success. In contrast, complaining, blaming, and finger pointing move you, your athletes, and your team toward unproductive performances. In simple terms, ruckus responses are distracting. Just listen to those individuals and teams that lose . . . most complain and blame others for their losses. Losers are good at "raising ruckus." However, raising ruckus is a waste of your time and energy. Your athletes (and team) need you to stay on task and stop the ruckus.

COACH UP Strategies

1. Admit your "ruckus." You must first come to terms with your own ruckus responses. This means being honest about how you respond to certain people, situations, and circumstances. No doubt you have opposing coaches and players, referees and umpires, as well as sporting venues that make it easy to justify arguing, complaining, and blaming. A bad call is easy to justify complaining about. It's also easy to justify blaming the outcome of games on the weather, travel schedules, court or field conditions, an injury, or lack of player personnel. Even if there is truth to your claims, it does your athletes little good to see or hear your ruckus. Take note of those people and situations that often lead you to start a ruckus. Then, be ready to change your responses. Your athletes need you to make these changes.

2. Change your "ruckus response." What your athletes see and hear . . . they will do and say. If you want your athletes to take responsibility for their performances and stay focused . . . you will have to take responsibility and stay focused. If you want them to remain calm and not argue . . . you will have to remain calm and not argue. When your athletes begin feeling "out of control" . . . they need to see you (their leader-coach) remain in control. They need to see you in control of your emotions and focused on the things that matter most. They need to see you in the moment, right here, right now, in control, and calmly focused on what to do next.

3. Be a "ruckus crusher." After taking control of your own ruckus, it will be important to turn your attention to your athletes. No doubt, some of your athletes *will* create ruckus. In fact, some athletes might create a lot of ruckus! These athletes often take little responsibility for their play, mistakes made, or their inappropriate responses to specific situations. Whether it's due to their immaturity, frustration, or because they are following the lead of a teammate or coach . . . these athletes will generally choose to *complain and blame* rather than take responsibility for their actions. This is where you have to step in and hold your athletes accountable to *"changing their ruckus responses."* Most athletes need reminded to "control the controllables" (see Rule 47). They need reminded that they cannot control referees and umpires, weather and playing conditions, or opponents' actions. What they can control is their own body, mind, and focus (see Rules 45-47). However, they will need your help in doing so. They need your help recognizing their ineffective behaviors (complaining and blaming) and replacing these behaviors with more appropriate thoughts and actions. Your athletes need help in "stopping the ruckus." Be a ruckus crusher. You'll be glad you did.

"It is not fair to ask of others what you are not willing to do yourself."

- Eleanor Roosevelt

Every word matters

"Many of life's failures are people who did not realize how close they were to success when they gave up."

- Thomas Edison

Every moment is an opportunity to make a positive impact on your athletes, fellow staff members, or anyone else associated with your program. Look for every opportunity to say something meaningful, empowering, motivating, or encouraging. The best coaches have a way of saying the right thing at just the right time . . . and when their athletes and staff need to hear it most. They are consistent with their "coaching messages" and they are trusted by their athletes to deliver these messages in a positive and uplifting way. Positive coaching is about practicing the *"Five I's."* In short, positive coaches regularly **IGNITE** passion, **INSTILL** confidence, **INSPIRE** commitment, **INTERJECT** positive leadership, and **INTEGRATE** effective and efficient team play. Your coaching should always promote trust, respect, belief, appreciation, pride, honor, admiration, and value. Look to create an "atmosphere" that embraces these qualities and characteristics. Below are 25 examples of short "lead in" phrases that can be used when communicating the *"Five I's."* Be creative in how you tailor these phrases so that you can *ignite, instill, inspire, interject, and integrate* your team toward victory. Every word does matter.

COACH UP Strategies

Empower and encourage your athletes today:

1. You're doing great . . .

2. I know you can do this . . .

3. I'm trusting you to get it done . . .

4. You're going to be fantastic . . .

5. I appreciate your efforts . . .

6. Great work . . .

7. I'm proud of you . . .

8. Keep fighting . . .

9. Yes *you can* . . . you got this . . .

10. It's great to coach you . . .

11. Push through it . . .

12. You *will* succeed . . .

13. You are so important to this team and our success . . .

14. I'm sorry . . . I was wrong . . . my bad . . . you were right . . .

15. I really respect and admire your (leadership, hard work, passion, intensity, focus, commitment, perseverance, etc.) . . .

16. You just keep improving . . . I cannot wait to see what you're going to do this upcoming season (pre-season, post-season, off-season) . . .

17. Your energy is contagious . . .

18. I love the positive influence you have on your teammates . . .

19. Keep working hard . . . it *will* come . . .

20. Your teammates need you . . . keep up the great leadership . . .

21. Try again . . . much better . . . keep going . . .

22. Fantastic . . . now go to the "next level" . . . take your team to the "next level" . . .

23. Dig deep . . . find a way . . . finish . . .

24. Nice job . . . outstanding . . .

25. Thank you . . . well done . . .

"A lot of people have gone further than they thought they could because someone else thought they could."

— **Unknown**

Do a little extra

"If you think small things don't matter, think of the last game you lost by one point."

- Anonymous

Sometimes doing a little extra produces big results. These "extras" are not difficult . . . they just take a little more time and demand a little more effort. It might be a phone call that you continue to put off, an email that needs to be "proofed" before sending, a word of encouragement to an athlete, one last review of a practice plan, a smile directed toward a staff member, or a surprise "thank you" note to an assistant coach for a job well done. Yes, the smallest things can sometimes produce the biggest results. In the end, some of your smallest actions, words, and gestures might have the greatest long-term impact on your athletes and staff. Your kind words, willingness to help, attention to detail, good attitude, positive demeanor, or simple "please" and "thank you" responses might be all it takes for someone to put forth more effort, maintain focus, or continue their good leadership. Athletes and coaches tend to work harder when they are treated nicely and know others care about them and have their best interest in mind. Doing a little extra may be the difference between your team *playing well . . .* and your team *winning.*

COACH UP Strategies

1. Look to compliment. Look for every opportunity to be kind. Encourage and compliment others when they least expect it. Surprise others with a sincere response of "nice job," "great work," "well done," "I appreciate your effort," or "I cannot do this without you." Be kind to and compliment others whenever possible.

> In a few short seconds, what and who you support, the words you speak, and how you choose to communicate have the potential to be available for all to see, read, and interpret.

2. Think again before you hit send. In the technology driven sport world, every form of communication (Myspace, LinkedIn, emails, texts, tweets, YouTube, Flickr, Facebook, blog posts, video feeds, Snapchat, Instagram, or any other form of social media sharing) is but one "click" away from becoming "front-page" news. In a few short seconds, what and who you support, the words you speak, and how you choose to communicate have the potential to be available for all to see, read, and interpret. So, re-read the email for proper wording and tone, think about how your text or tweet message might be perceived, be sure your blog is promoting what you really want it to, think again about the pictures you are about to post, consider who might read what you are sending, and double check that you are sending things to the right "recipients." Stop, double check, and think again before you hit send.

3. Check your "athlete suggestion box." Consider allowing your athletes the opportunity to make suggestions (i.e., via a suggestion box outside the locker room, team room, or your office) for improving the team. Make it clear that the suggestion box is not for "complaining" or "venting" about things not liked. It's for sharing new ideas on how to improve the team. Maybe it's a change in how coaches and athletes are communicating, a variation in how a practice is conducted, or a better way to motivate and empower team members. Whatever the suggestion, athletes should be specific, as well as willing to provide a clear rationale for what they are suggesting. In the end, if you are asking for (and accepting) suggestions, be willing to implement something being suggested. When an athlete suggests something beneficial or offers constructive input that might improve the team . . . be willing to give it a try.

> When an athlete suggests something beneficial or offers constructive input that might improve the team . . . be willing to give it a try.

4. Remember . . . every person matters. Everyone has something to offer the team. Look to treat all team members with respect and dignity. Be purposeful in making positive impressions with every athlete and staff member. Think about your athletes, coaches, medical staff, administrative staff, athletic directors, and anyone else associated with your team. Everyone does matter and they need to feel like they do.

5. Appreciate the little changes. At the end of each day, list one positive change taking place . . . then take time to appreciate what you have listed. Did an athlete compliment your coaching? Is an athlete's attitude getting better? Are your athletes more responsive to your coaching demands? Are your team captains "stepping up" and improving their leadership? Are your athletes starting to understand their roles and responsibilities? Is your team developing trust and togetherness? Is your staff more efficient and productive? Whatever was positive today, be sure to acknowledge it. At the end of the day, appreciate the little things.

> Make genuine connections, talk about "real stuff," and build positive relationships.

6. Connect. Learn as much as you can about your athletes (see Rule 29). Learn the names of brothers, sisters, moms, dads, and grandparents. Mark your calendar with birthdays and celebrate important events in your athletes' lives. Talk to your athletes with a purpose of really getting to know them. Ask specific questions about family, friends, boyfriends, girlfriends, roommates, career aspirations, travel dreams, favorite foods, pets, music, and movies. Engage your athletes in meaningful conversations. Make genuine connections, talk about "real stuff," and build positive relationships.

7. Do a little more *and* complete the job. Do more than what is expected and follow-through with what you promised. Stay a little longer and come a little earlier. Do a little more preparing, encouraging, strategizing, and supporting. "Stand out" from every other coach and always show your commitment to your athletes and staff. In the end, doing a little more and completing the job gives others good reason to trust you . . . and trust is the foundation of every great team (see Rule 5 and 29).

8. Make a list and check it twice. Make a list for everything that needs completed today. Prioritize all phone calls, emails, and text reminders to be completed and sent today. Check that all scheduled time-frames and appointments are realistic. Ask if the correct room was reserved for the team meeting and if your updated practice plan was received by your coaches. Question yourself and question others. Ask if everyone has completed their duties and if everyone is ready to go. Make a list and check it twice . . . before you start.

9. Show first. Show more than you tell. Yes, people need to hear that you care about, are concerned about, respect, and appreciate them. But more than anything, they need to "see" these things. So, smile, offer a "fist-pump," "high-five," or give a "thumbs up." People are more in tune with what you show them than what you tell them. Your facial expressions, body language, behaviors, and actions are more important than you might think. In time, your athletes and staff will believe what they see more than what they hear. Remember, one positive gesture can go a long way in terms of commitment, trust, and motivation. What you show is more important than what you tell.

10. Tune in to what is not said. Be sure to take note of what your athletes are saying . . . *when they are not talking.* Notice the subtle cues of a fearful look, a distressed smile, apprehensive body language, a walk that lacks confidence, decreased intensity and effort, or a lack of passion or joy. These "cues" say a lot. Address your athlete's nonverbal cues with sincerity and concern. Err on the side of showing your athletes that you care. Ask them how they are doing *and* what you can do to help.

"I've learned that people will forget what you said, people will forget what you did, but people will never forget how you made them feel."

- Maya Angelou

Rise above the rest

"Hold yourself responsible for a higher standard than anyone else expects of you. Never excuse yourself."

- Henry Ward Beecher (US Congregational Minister, 1813-1887)

Make it a goal to be better than the rest. When others are negative, be positive. When others are bad-mouthing the administration, re-direct the conversation toward something more encouraging and productive. When others engage in constant complaining about "what's wrong," find a solution to the problem. When others focus on a bad call or play, focus on the next play, series,

> Move ahead of everyone else, move beyond the current situation, and move on from where you are now.

or trip down the field or up the court. And when others are "shutting down" and talking about what can't be done, *rise above the rest* to lead your athletes, staff, and team to accomplish what can be done. Move ahead of everyone else, move beyond the current situation, and move on from where you are now. Stay out-front of your competition. Your team will not benefit from you or your players getting "bogged-down" with any form of bad-mouthing, negativism, or talking about what cannot be done (see Rule 8). Coach up! Rise above the rest . . . and be better than the rest!

COACH UP Strategies

1. Spend time with positive people. You are who you spend time with. Why spend time with people who bring you down, rarely smile or laugh, lack enthusiasm, or find it hard to offer encouraging words? Why not spend time with positive, enthusiastic, happy, supportive people who are open to you and your coaching ideas? It's simple . . . the company you keep will "bring you down" or "lift you up." Choose to be "lifted up." Hang out with people that have positive things to say, want to be challenged, want to improve, and who respond well to your positive ways. Hang out with people who "add value" to you and can help you be a better coach. If you want to be a positive coach . . . spend time with positive people.

2. Just be nice. If you can't say anything nice then don't say anything at all. It's easy to be critical, point out the bad, and focus on the negative. In contrast, it can be hard to remain positive, point out the good in someone, and focus on the positive aspects in a given situation. It is human nature to focus on what went wrong, what others can't do, are not doing, and cannot do well. However, there is always something positive that can be highlighted. Yes, that's right. There is always some good to be found. One of your many coaching jobs is to find that good, talk about it, and build on it whenever possible. Stop all bad-mouthing, back-stabbing, and critical coaching (see Rule 42). These things only serve to alienate and isolate those you coach. *People like being around nice people and they tend to gravitate toward those who are nice.* Find something nice to say and something positive, upbeat, and encouraging to draw attention to. And don't forget to say *"please," "thank you," "no thank you," and "I'm sorry."*

3. Get ahead and stay ahead. Never stop coaching! Always look for opportunities to get ahead of your competition and "take the next step." Never stand still. Move to the next thing, organize the next practice, make the next phone call, watch the next film, design the next play, and make the next visit. It's not enough to simply get through the day, practice, or week. Any coach can do that. To get ahead . . . you need to do "extra." To stay ahead, you need to do even more. When other coaches are looking at what is next . . . *focus on "what is after what is next."* Study more, read more, watch more, and ask more questions. Think one or two steps ahead of everyone else. Never stop growing and improving. Act now to get ahead *and* stay ahead.

4. Stumble forward. When you stumble . . . stumble forward. When you make mistakes and fail . . . learn from your mistakes, stay positive, continue to take responsibility, and persevere through the stumbles. Keep moving forward. In most cases, your stumbles will not define you

> ## What you do after you stumble is what really counts.

or your coaching career. However, what you do after you stumble often defines who you are as a coach. Mistakes and failures are a part of life. What you do after you stumble is what really counts. Rise above your stumbles. Whatever went wrong is temporary and will not last long. Get back on task and keep moving forward.

"Make a game of finding something positive in every situation."

- Brian Tracy

Winners win

"A competitor will find a way to win. Competitors take bad breaks and use them to drive themselves just that much harder. Quitters take bad breaks and use them as reasons to give up. It's all a matter of pride."

- Nancy Lopez

It's great to be around winners. Winners just have a way about them that makes you want to watch, listen, and admire. They tend to look at the "bright side" of things, remain positive in the face of obstacles, and keep an optimistic outlook for the future. In contrast, losers would rather whine, complain, and focus on what is wrong with their current situations. In short, winners spend most

> In short, winners spend most of their time working and training and losers spend most of their time whining and complaining.

of their time working and training and losers spend most of their time whining and complaining. Winners regularly take responsibility for their behaviors, change perspective when needed, and have a clear purpose for what they think, say, and do. Winners win because they spend their time focused on being productive. Losers spend most of their time being unproductive. The reality of most sport teams is that they contain both winners *and* losers. Some athletes whine, while others stay focused on what it takes to win. Similarly, some coaches spend too much time complaining about bad calls, lazy athletes, a lack of facilities, and little support from the administration. To be honest, many athletes and coaches whine and complain too much! Yet, winning coaches focus on *"things that matter"* and make the best of their situations and resources, and in doing so, move toward creating a winning culture, winning athletes, and a winning team. The goal is to win . . . but to win you must be willing to think, act, respond, and lead like a winner. Winners win. Whine less if you want to win more!

COACH UP Strategies

1. Plan to win. Approach all situations believing that a positive outcome will result and expect your staff and team to do everything possible to produce a win. Although the outcome is never a guarantee, always prepare for and plan on winning.

2. Stop whining. Just "do the job" . . . no whining. Develop the confidence, persistence, and perseverance to outlast others who whine and give up. If you don't get the results you are looking for then try again, try something new, or change the plan in order to reach the goal. Keep going until the task is completed as planned. Do your job . . . without whining or complaining!

3. Promote the positive. Make a point to talk about the good things that are happening and what your athletes and other coaches are doing well. Encourage and esteem those you interact with and refuse to speak badly about others. Focus on the positive and the good. At the end of each day, acknowledge those people for whom you are most grateful.

> Be willing to work harder, think bigger, read more, change old ways of doing things, or be pushed outside your comfort zone.

4. Talk about getting better. Talk about what "could be," what "might be," and what "will be." Ask questions that challenge your athletes and team to think outside the box and beyond the current situation. Be willing to work harder, think bigger, read more, change old ways of doing things, or be pushed outside your comfort zone. When others spend time with you they should know that you want to get better, be better, and do better. Athletes get excited about getting better . . . and the chance to be a winner!

5. Give the credit. Winning coaches should look for every opportunity to promote their athletes, team, and staff. Give credit whenever possible. It's the sign of a winner . . . and it's just good coaching.

"A winning effort begins with preparation."

- Joe Gibbs

It's all about the coach

"Will you look back on life and say, 'I wish I had', or 'I'm glad I did'?"

- Zig Ziglar

Coaching is all about helping others succeed. It's about directing individuals and groups toward achieving an agreed upon standard or goal. It's about mentoring, teaching, encouraging, and correcting others. Coaching is about taking care of others . . . sometimes at the expense of taking care of you. Your athletes, staff, and team need you to lead, manage, teach, mentor, guide, direct, and defend them every day. *They need you to be your best every day.* But to consistently be your best, you will have to take care of yourself for the long-term. If you don't take care of yourself, you cannot take care of others. Don't neglect your teams' most valuable resource . . . *you!* Your team needs you to take care of yourself so that you can take care of them. They are counting on you . . . to take care of you!

COACH UP Strategies

1. Improve your health and fitness. Take time to assess your own health and fitness habits. Follow-through with your yearly medical check-ups and keep a watchful eye on blood pressure and cholesterol levels . . . and don't forget to schedule your yearly mammogram or prostate screening. In addition, be sure to "practice what you preach" in terms of regular exercise, proper nutrition, and adequate sleep. Take care of yourself so that you are healthy, alert, and focused every day.

2. Reduce your stress. Take note of those people and situations that cause you the most stress. You have to know the source of your stress before you can reduce your stress. You cannot change most people or situations . . . so in terms of managing your coaching stress . . . any change must come from you. For example, you might change the amount of time you spend around specific people, how much you allow yourself to engage them in conversation, or how you respond to them. Managing your stress could mean eating better, exercising more, getting more sleep, or delegating selected leadership responsibilities to other staff members. You might also have to change how you think about some athletes, other coaches,

> You cannot change most people or situations . . . so in terms of managing your coaching stress . . . any change must come from you.

your administration, the media, wins and losses, as well as various other coaching situations that cause you stress and anxiety. *Stress is cumulative!* This means your stress increases over the course of a week, month, or season. Your "coaching stresses" need your direct and immediate attention. Determine what changes are needed to better manage your stress . . . and begin reducing your stress today.

3. Empty the trash. Get rid of everything that is not helping you improve. Simplify your coaching. The saying, "*less is more*" is often true. Don't waste time, energy, or coaching opportunities doing things that don't work and don't matter. Throw out what needs thrown out. Tweak or "makeover" any coaching practices, rules, roles, or expectations (see Rule 6). Get rid of the "stuff" that no longer works and old ways of doing things. Empty the trash. Everything you do, say, and expect should have a clear purpose.

4. Work smarter. Work harder than everyone else . . . but work smarter too. Continue to invest in what is most important and most worthy of your time (see Rule 28). You get to pick what is modeled, expected, reinforced, and rewarded. In short, you pick the team climate and the standard by which everyone is held accountable. Think before you speak, respond, or act. Be smart about what you are saying and doing.

5. Be consistent. Be consistent with who you are, how you act and respond, and what others can expect from you. Bring your best . . . and make sure your coaching is a set of consistent behaviors that others can expect and rely on each day, week, practice, and competition. Be consistent in all you do.

"And in the end, it's not the years in your life that count. It's the life in your years."

- Abraham Lincoln

The Rules of Motivation

Motivation starts with a clearly stated *intent*

"Knowledge alone is not enough to get desired results. You must have the more elusive ability to teach and to motivate. This defines a leader; if you can't teach and you can't motivate, you can't lead."

- John Wooden

At the core of all great performances is one's motivation to perform the task. Numerous factors impact motivation (e.g., sleep, nutrition, the sport environment, athlete personality, coaching influence, history of successes and failures, and team dynamics), but one's intent for doing something may be the most important factor to consider when assessing motivation. How many times have you heard athletes grumble, "What are we doing?" "Why do we have to do this?" If your athletes are unclear about *what* to do or *why* they are being asked to do something, they will probably lack the correct motivation to do their best. A lot of factors impact motivation . . . but motivation begins with a clearly stated intent for completing the task.

Intent - is the thought behind a goal. Intent can be geared toward the process (strategies for improving) or the outcome (strategies for winning). No doubt, goals can be beneficial in directing actions (see Rule 18) but if athletes do not clearly understand ***why*** they are engaging in a particular movement (skill or drill) or ***what*** is to be accomplished by the movement, the desired result (goal) is often difficult to achieve. *Make sure your athletes know what you want . . . and why?* The same drill or exercise (movement), completed with different intentions (e.g., speed vs. force vs. accuracy or "do your best" vs. "beat your best time"), can lead to very different performance outcomes. Clearly communicate the desired intent for what you are asking your athletes to do. What do you intend your athletes to accomplish from each drill, exercise, set, or workout?

COACH UP Strategies

1. Assess current skill sets. Assess your athletes in the area of *technical skills* (e.g., passing, rebounding, catching, shooting, blocking, defending), *fundamental abilities* (e.g., power, quickness, vertical jump, speed, agility, flexibility), *psychological skills* (e.g., handling pressure, directing focus, gaining confidence, overcoming mistakes, remaining optimistic), or any combination of the above.

2. Design specific drills and exercises (or even an entire training program) to address the needed skills. For example, if the goal is to improve technical skills, then tailor training exercises (practices and drills) to optimize and improve specific offensive or defensive skill sets. If the goal is to improve psychological skills, coordinate a training program to improve confidence and mental toughness, develop strategies to handle pressure, or redirect focus after a mistake (see Rules 45-49).

3. Answer all questions. Do your best to answer any and all questions that your athletes may have about the purpose of a practice, drill, team meeting, film session, travel schedule, conditioning program, or anything else associated with training and competing. Be clear as to when and where and how things are to be done. To start, it is always important to explain how . . . *how* to carry out a specific role, *how* to communicate, *how* to lead, or *how* to play with the desired attitude, intensity, or focus. In addition, many athletes will need to be reminded of *how* to act, *how* to dress, *where* to meet, *where* to sit, *when* to arrive, *when* to get ready, *what* to say, and *what* to eat. And some athletes, depending on age and skill level, will also need reminded as to *why* a specific position (spot) on a field or court is important, *why* a drill is designed the way it is, and *why* the role expectations are what they are. No doubt, your athletes will have many questions. Be sure to answer what, when, where, how, and why?

> Be sure to answer what, when, where, how, and why?

"There's always the motivation of wanting to win. Everybody has that. But a champion needs a motivation above and beyond winning."

- Pat Riley

Motivation is enhanced by well-defined *effort*

"The successful person makes a habit of doing what the failing person doesn't like to do."

- Thomas Edison

Once a clear intent is stated (***what*** is to be done and ***why***), your athletes must then agree to put forth the maximum **effort** needed to accomplish the task and reach the desired outcome.

Effort – is simply the amount of work one is willing to put forth to complete a task. Assuming the athlete has the proper intent (i.e., they know *what* to do and *why* they are doing it) he or she must then be able *and* willing to put forth the effort required. Many athletes simply do not know what it will take to reach their goals or how much effort it will take to accomplish the desired outcome. As a result, athletes often need help clarifying how much work is required to complete the task. Some athletes may also need the correct effort "modeled" so that they can "see" what appropriate effort looks like given the task and your coaching expectations.

COACH UP Strategies

1. Talk about how much effort is required to perform the desired task. Be specific in discussing how much effort is needed to reach the desired outcome. Quantify the effort whenever possible by providing time frames, monthly projections, expected training days, gym hours needed, number of shots to be taken, sets and reps to be completed, miles per week, yardage per day, or daily training times expected for off-season conditioning. In addition, provide sport examples (i.e., stories, videos, movies, or guest speakers) that promote, define, and clarify the "standard effort" you are asking for.

> When possible, model the correct speed, intensity, effort, quickness, power, or explosiveness.

2. Model (show) what the appropriate effort looks like. What does the appropriate intensity in practice look like? What does the correct effort in competition look like? When possible, model the correct speed, intensity, effort, quickness, power, or explosiveness. If you cannot model it yourself, highlight a current athlete or team member that regularly displays the correct effort and intensity you want. If you do not have a current role-model athlete, find a model athlete on a video or YouTube clip. Do whatever is needed to *show* your athletes what the appropriate effort looks like.

3. Associate hard work with fun. Help your athletes "see" and "feel" the enjoyment that can come from working hard and attaining an agreed upon goal. Equate working hard with feeling good. Help your athletes make the connection between hard work, commitment, sacrifice, goal attainment, satisfaction, and a sense of accomplishment. Working hard to attain a goal should be rewarding and fulfilling. Talk it, show it, feel it, and celebrate it.

> Help your athletes make the connection between hard work, commitment, sacrifice, goal attainment, satisfaction, and a sense of accomplishment.

"The six W's . . . work will win when wishing won't."
- Todd Blackledge

Motivation is maintained with a specific *focus*

"We want to practice better than anyone has ever practiced before."

- Pete Carroll

With a clearly stated **intent** and a well-defined **effort**, it is imperative that your athletes now develop and maintain the right **focus** of attention. If you put it all together, *motivation = intent + effort + focus.*

Focus – is the athlete's attention to specific cues. These cues can be *internal* (e.g., thoughts, emotions, or physical responses like heart rate

> In terms of focus, it is most important to determine what cues are relevant for the given task and then attend to those cues as needed.

and respiration rate) or *external* (e.g., a ball, line, net, or teammate). Cues can further be divided into *relevant* (cues that direct one to successful performance outcomes) or *irrelevant* (cues that become distractions and prevent successful performance outcomes). To successfully execute a skill, a focus on specific external-relevant cues in the environment (e.g., a trajectory of a ball, the position of an opponent, the sound of a starter gun) is best. In terms of focus, it is most important to determine what cues are relevant for the given task and then attend to those cues as needed. A focus on relevant cues leads to better performance outcomes. Better outcomes lead to enhanced motivations. Maximize and maintain your athletes' motivations by helping them focus on relevant cues.

COACH UP Strategies

1. Clarify the proper focus. What kind of focus is needed in order to be successful? What should your athletes focus on? What should they think about? Is there a need for an internal focus? How about an external focus? And what might impact their ability to refocus? Help your athletes determine the proper focus given the tasks to be completed.

2. Determine relevant cues. When attended to, these *relevant cues* will increase the likelihood of performance success. These cues should directly relate to refining a skill, as well as completing the task given the athlete's unique skill set. Examples of relevant focus cues might include back of the rim, hands out front, elbow down, head up, feet shoulder width apart, eyes up field, low post, blue line, stick up, square to target, first down marker, or 8 meter arc.

3. Develop specific "cue words" or "cue phrases." Establish cue words and phrases that will help your athletes develop and maintain an **external** and **relevant** focus of attention. For example, a cue word or phrase might be *ball, hands, rim, relax, fire, explode, power, shuffle, smooth, fly, gentle, switch, eyes, spot, line, swivel, pivot, check, turn and go, step and throw, quick feet, or soft off glass.* These are words that can be repeated silently or out loud. They can be tailored for an individual athlete or they can be adopted and used by an offense, defense, or the entire team. Whatever the cue word or phrase, it should promote an immediate, specific, and relevant focus of attention (see Rule 47 for more on sharpening focus and developing mental toughness skills). Remember, **motivation = intent + effort + focus.**

"We just want to win. That's the bottom line. I think a lot of times people may become content with one championship or a little bit of success, but we don't really reflect on what we've done in the past. We focus on the present."

- Derek Jeter

Purpose leads to long-term motivation

"Motivation is fire from within. If someone else tries to light that fire under you, chances are it will burn very briefly."

-Stephen R. Covey

Finding what motivates one athlete (or your entire team), at just the right time, can be difficult. Motivation takes insight (a plan) and patience (time). There are many ways to motivate your athletes, but motivation strategies often fall into three categories; *instilling fear, offering incentives,* or *providing a sense of purpose.* Fear and incentives are typically "short-term motivators," whereas providing

> Athletes motivated by fear are more likely to focus on avoiding behaviors (e.g., losing a position or making a mistake) than achieving desired outcomes (e.g., playing well and improving a skill).

purpose (or meaning) is more long-term. The challenge is finding what motivates who, and when, and where, and why.

Instilling **fear** is simple (and it *can* quickly motivate some athletes) but over time, fear can easily lead to resentment and disloyalty. Athletes motivated by fear are more likely to focus on avoiding behaviors (e.g., losing a position or making a mistake) than achieving desired outcomes (e.g., playing well and improving a skill). These athletes typically focus on what *not to do*, rather than what *to do*. Over time, stress builds . . . as does a growing sense of resentment and disloyalty toward the one instilling the fear.

Incentives too can be effective for the short-term. Dangling the "carrot" (e.g., playing time, the status of a starting role, money, trophies, etc.) is a strong motivator for many athletes but these extrinsic means generally last for only a short time before the "incentives" need increased or made more appealing. The less appealing the incentive, the less motivation one shows. In contrast, more valued incentives yield more motivation . . . at least until the incentive is no longer valued.

For most athletes, developing a sense of **purpose** is most effective for promoting long-term motivation. Creating a sense of purpose is about changing the way athletes think about their roles, their reasons for coming to practice, their influence on teammates, their membership on the team, and their reasons for playing and competing. Providing purpose and meaning is about creating an environment that is conducive to personal growth, as well as an environment that encourages athletes to motivate themselves and their teammates. Developing purpose and meaning takes more time, energy, and coach investment but it will likely lead to greater *long-term athlete motivation*.

No doubt, there are many ways to motivate your athletes. Throughout a season, you will likely use motivation strategies from all three categories. However, the goal should be to develop long-term motivation by creating practice and competitive climates that are meaningful and provide a clear sense of purpose.

COACH UP Strategies

1. Get input from your leaders. Ask your athletes (especially your team leaders) if what you are saying and doing is motivating. Encourage your leaders to make suggestions about how day-to-day activities (e.g., pre and post-practice talks, practice schedules, travel itineraries, game day preparations, response to mistakes, and overall coach-athlete communication, etc.) might be improved and made more meaningful. Be willing to incorporate something new or make a change based on what you are hearing from your leaders.

2. Give your athletes a reason to work hard. Invest extra time to develop sincere and trusting relationships with your players (see Rule 5 and 29). Athletes will work harder (and longer) for a coach who they know genuinely believes in them, cares about them, and is committed to helping them achieve their potential. At the heart of player motivation . . . is the quality of the coach-athlete relationship.

> At the heart of player motivation . . . is the quality of the coach-athlete relationship.

3. Model what you want to see. Be motivated yourself. If you want your athletes to work hard, you better be working hard. If you want your athletes to put in extra time, you better be putting in extra time. Athletes do what they see. This is why the motivation of the coaching staff is so important and why it is important to have quality team leaders who can lead by example, hold accountable, and promote a climate of motivation and hard work. Set a motivational "standard" by what you do, say, and expect. Say it, expect it, and make sure *you* do it!

> Positive words create action . . . and action leads to desired outcomes!

4. Catch your athletes (and staff) doing things right. Athletes love to hear what they are doing well. Positive words are encouraging and generally lead to greater commitment and effort. Positive words create action . . . and action leads to desired outcomes! Go out of your way to notice your athletes correctly doing something. Find someone doing something right . . . and let them know it!

5. Remember, both situations <u>and</u> people motivate. Do your best to create a "motivational climate" but also take time to select and maintain the best personnel for that climate. Motivated people like to spend time with motivated people. Whenever possible, match your athletes based on their personalities and motivation for a given task. Motivation is contagious and the motivation of one or two athletes can quickly spread to create positive team momentum.

6. Acknowledge process before outcome. Effort, hard work, intensity, passion, commitment, and attitude are controllable aspects of every performance. Acknowledge these aspects and encourage your athletes to be consistent in how they prepare for and perform each day. No doubt the final outcome is important. However, acknowledge the process (i.e., effort, hard work, intensity, passion, etc.) before the outcome!

"Find your passion and make it happen. Be on a mission and live your life of purpose. Be motivated by your desire to achieve rather than your fear of failure."

-Gary Mack

"Goal-Get"

"Setting a goal is not the main thing. It is deciding how you will go about achieving it and staying with the plan."

- Tom Landry

Well planned goals can help many athletes narrow focus, overcome distractions, work smarter, persevere, and improve performances. Yet, the process of goal-setting can be frustrating. For many athletes and coaches, there is often too much talk about goal-setting and too little "action" toward attaining the goal. In short, there is too much talk and not enough action. Goal-setting is about a dream.

> A good *goal plan* is one that has a good *action plan.*

Goal attainment is about achieving that dream. Dreaming is easy but achieving the dream can be hard. Goal-attainment is an ***action process***, and most athletes need help in developing the action strategies that enable them to *"goal-get"* (and reach) their targeted dreams. They understand the importance of goals but do not understand what it takes to goal-get. A good *goal plan* is one that has a good *action plan.* Help your athletes take action and ***"Goal-Get"*** their target goals.

COACH UP Strategies

1. Define the goal. Be specific in terms of the target goal. Target goals should be clearly defined and include how goal progress will be measured. All available resources (i.e., facilities, personnel, support networks, etc.) that impact goal attainment, as well as realistic time frames for accomplishing the goals, must be understood. Be clear about the efforts needed from others (e.g., cooperation and contributions from coaches and teammates), as well as all daily, weekly, and monthly "deadlines" for completing the targeted goals.

2. Determine what will be sacrificed. What price will be paid? To reach the target goal, what is the athlete willing to sacrifice (give up) or change? For example, reaching a target goal might entail an athlete sacrificing part of his or her social life, changing nutrition habits, or committing more time to off-season strength and conditioning programs. It might also mean changing one's attitude, work ethic, character, or decision-making. Whatever the sacrifices, they must be made known, understood, and then accepted.

3. Create an action plan. *This is most important!* Determine exactly **how** the target goal will be reached. What *action strategies* must be completed to "goal-get"? If the athlete needs to commit more . . . how do they do this? What does it look like to commit more at practice? What does greater commitment look like in the off-season? What does commitment look like in terms of more in-season mental training, doing extra workouts each week, or changing a diet? What about one's attitude? How does one go about changing an attitude? And what about changing character? How does someone go about improving character and making better decisions? Help your athletes answer these questions as they develop "action steps" for reaching their target goals.

> Encourage them through difficult times and point out previous sacrifices made, goals already attained, and growth toward the targeted goal.

4. Prioritize what is first. What needs done first? Some athletes will need help with determining a target goal and some will need help with prioritizing the action strategies for reaching their goal. And some athletes may simply need guidance in restructuring and better managing their days, in order to carry out their new action plans. What needs done first? Maybe it's deciding on a workout partner, a place and time to meet, or a way to ensure accountability. Goal priorities are often based on goal importance, available resources, personnel, and time constraints. Be sure to prioritize the action plan . . . but start with what needs done first.

5. Encourage the goal-get process. Encourage and support your athletes in reaching their targeted goals. Help your athletes stay on task and focused on the important action strategies. Encourage them through difficult times and point out previous sacrifices made, goals already attained, and growth toward the targeted goal. Your encouragement and support will likely be needed throughout the entire *goal-get* process.

6. Hold accountable. There will be "lapses" in motivation. When these days arrive for your athletes, be there to hold them accountable to what they set out to accomplish. Remind and refocus them on the targeted goal and the action plan they committed to. Help them re-prioritize what needs done today so that they can get back on track for reaching their goals. Keep pushing them to *"goal-get"* and reach their target goals.

"We need to know where we are going, and how we plan to get there. Our dreams and aspirations must be translated into real and tangible goals, with priorities and a time frame."

- Merlin Olsen

Inspire your people

"If your actions inspire others to dream more, learn more, do more, and become more, you are a leader."

- John Quincy Adams

In simple terms, you motivate your athletes when you inspire performance. Some of your athletes are motivated by ***challenge***. These athletes are typically inspired by challenging situations or challenging words. In contrast you have some athletes who thrive on ***recognition***, or a formal act of ***appreciation***. For these athletes, motivation stems primarily from positive words in the form of

> Motivation is unique to the individual but your athletes are motivated and inspired by your words, your actions, and the sporting environments you create.

recognition in front of their peers *or* appreciation expressed during one-on-one coach-athlete interactions. You also have athletes motivated by situations that allow for opportunities to produce **quality** performances. These athletes are inspired by any opportunity to showcase their skills and talents and are most motivated to "show" their coaches and teammates what they are capable of doing. And finally, you have some athletes that are simply motivated by the **status** of being on a team. For these athletes, motivation comes from their ongoing affiliation with a team and being recognized as an "athlete." They are motivated by the social status of maintaining team membership, interacting with teammates, and proudly wearing all team clothing (e.g., sweats, jerseys, uniform, team jacket, shoes, hats, etc.). Obviously, athlete motivations vary, and although it takes extra time on your part, it is important that you know your athletes' primary motives for practicing and performing. Motivation is unique to the individual but your athletes are motivated and inspired by your words, your actions, and the sporting environments you create.

COACH UP Strategies

1. Create challenges. For those athletes that thrive on a challenge, match them with teammates who also want to be challenged. Your most competitive athletes usually want to be challenged. So, whenever possible, pit one against another (1 vs. 1) or one group against another group (3 on 3). Challenge your most competitive soccer players with continuous 1v1 drills or create sub-teams to compete in a "best of five" shootout. How about challenging your most competitive basketball players to a "best of 25" free throw competition at the end of practice. Or challenge your top tennis players to be the first to 50 volleys without an error. Remember your high challenge athletes will need highly competitive and challenging practice drills and situations every day (see Rule 50 for more on molding consistent competitors).

2. Recognize (and *maybe* reward). Some athletes thrive on recognition. These athletes respond best to positive verbal feedback and often look to their coaches for recognition of their work ethic and commitment. The most desired recognition is often verbal praise that is "handed out" in the presence of teammates. For example, recognizing a player's positive leadership following a game or practice could be extremely motivating for a team captain. For another athlete, it might be important to recognize a positive attitude, an appropriate response to a mistake, or a commitment level that is "above and beyond" the rest of the team. In some situations, you might also provide a "reward" (e.g., playing time, honorary captain, a starting role, etc.) as an added means of recognition. However, be careful with rewards. Once you start rewarding your athletes . . . they may start looking for (and expecting) a similar reward in the future. Be careful not to start a reward structure that you cannot continue to provide as the season progresses.

3. Verbalize your appreciation. Rather than formal recognition (in front of peers), some athletes need reassurance that they are appreciated by their coaches and teammates. A simple "thank you" away from the rest of the team is sometimes all it takes. For example, as you leave practice you can thank your senior captain for a much appreciated model of intensity and hard work. In the same way, you can

> A "thank you," "good job," and "I really appreciate what you bring to this team," can go a long way in motivating some athletes.

call an athlete into your office with the sole intent of communicating your appreciation for a positive attitude "off the bench." A "thank you," "good job," and "I really appreciate what you bring to this team," can go a long way in motivating some athletes. It may not seem like a big deal to you, but verbalizing your appreciation can be powerful and very motivating. Your words do matter (see Rule 9).

4. Allow for mastery and quality. Some athletes are primarily motivated to improve their skills and "do a good job." In fact, for some athletes improving their individual performances may be more important than winning. These athletes need opportunities to improve and enhance their previous best performances. Their motivations rest in wanting to "do better than last time." Their goal is to "get better every day." They are looking to master their sport skills. If they win . . . great! But getting better and "self-improving" are the primary motives behind their practicing and training. For these athletes, it is important to create practice opportunities where they can attempt to meet and exceed their last performance. They need regular opportunities to assess their own mastery and quality of performance.

5. Encourage autonomy. Encourage your athletes to "think for themselves" as they find ways to complete the required tasks. Be clear with what you expect but give your athletes the freedom to do what is needed to reach the goal. Think autonomy, creativity, and freedom of choice as your athletes "master" and refine their skills. The more you trust your athletes to "get the job done" . . . the more intrinsic desire, passion, and mastery motivation you will likely promote. Many of your athletes already have (or will soon have) the needed skills to successfully complete the task. At some point you will need to get out of the way and trust your athletes to finish the job.

> At some point you will need to get out of the way and trust your athletes to finish the job.

"I was successful because you believed in me."

- Ulysses S. Grant, to Abraham Lincoln

The Rules of Team Building

Start your team *forming*

"Coming together is a beginning. Keeping together is progress. Working together is success."

- Henry Ford

Sport teams are a lot like "family." Family members are forced to regularly interact with one another, make decisions, resolve conflicts, take on new responsibilities, and be held accountable. Teams too must learn to work together despite some team members' opposing views and opinions. In the end, however, teammates must learn to trust one another, cooperate in difficult times,

> In reality, excitement about the upcoming season is high but knowledge of what to do is often low.

and develop a "synergy" directed toward a common team goal.

Although each team is unique in regard to membership, motivation, team dynamics, leadership, and communication, it is generally accepted that **teams progress through specific developmental stages** over the course of a season. Most teams can expect to **form, storm, norm,** and then **perform.**[1]

How long your team remains in each stage (or if your team makes it to the next stage) depends on many factors. Your team is dynamic (always changing) and you must be prepared to coach your team through each stage. Successful teams do not happen by chance. They are developed over time and led by a coach who understands the *"growth of a team"* and who can provide effective coach leadership across all four stages. As your season progresses, each stage will demand a different coaching style.[2] As the season begins, you will have to start your team forming.[1]

Forming. As the word implies, this is the beginning stage for your team. This stage might be referred to as the *dependency stage* because team members are often dependent on one another and you (their coach) for a sense of direction. It could also be called the *orientation stage*[2] since team members are looking to be "oriented" to one another, the team structure, various team rules, and what might be expected of them at team gatherings and practices. Although this stage includes many activities (and a lot of excitement about completing tasks), there may be little productive work being accomplished. In reality, excitement about the upcoming season is high but knowledge of what to do is often low.

COACH UP Strategies

1. Tell them what to do. The *"telling leadership style"* is most needed during the *forming* stage of group development.[3] In this stage, team members spend much of their time getting to know one another, their coaching staff, as well as the various rules, norms, and overall team structure. As already stated, this is an exciting time for most athletes but team productivity can be minimal. With many unanswered questions (early in the season), it will be important for you to *"tell them what to do."* Clearly outline individual and team goals, individual roles, team rules, and overall team expectations. Although they are likely getting a lot of support from their teammates, they are unsure what to do. Be direct in telling your athletes "what" you want and "when" you want it.

> Be direct in telling your athletes "what" you want and "when" you want it.

2. Keep your expectations in check. As stated, when your team is forming, most of your athletes are unclear about what to do, how to perform their roles, what is expected in terms of team norms, and who can be trusted. As a result, they are often not yet able to effectively communicate with one another or productively work together. Don't expect too much until you are clear with (and your athletes understand) what, when, where, and how you want things done.

3. Help your athletes answer the following questions. *What is our (team) purpose? How do we work together? What is my role in helping this team come together? How are things going to be organized? How do we best communicate? What can I expect from the team leaders?*

What can I expect from my coaches? At this stage, the intent is to clearly outline a team purpose, the organization and structure to accomplish that purpose, as well as all coaching expectations for reaching team goals.

4. Make it fun. Okay, I'm stating the obvious . . . but don't forget that your sport (and your coaching) is meant to be fun. The beginning of each season should be fun and exciting. Laugh and joke with your athletes. Set the tone for a fun season by developing meaningful (fun) relationships. Enjoy your new team. Spend time having fun!

"Great beginnings are not as important as the way one finishes."

- Dr. James Dobson

1 Tuckman, B. (1965). Developmental sequence in small groups. *Psychological Bulletin, 63,* 384-399.

2 Blanchard, K., Carew, D., & Parisi-Carew, E. (2009). *The one minute manager builds high-performing teams (revised and updated).* William Morrow.

3 Hersey, P., Blanchard, K., & Johnson, D. (2012). *Management of organizational behavior (10th ed.).* Prentice-Hall.

Prepare for team *storming*

"In a crisis, don't hide behind anything or anybody. They are going to find you anyway."

- Paul Bear Bryant

Storming. Although healthy (and beneficial) to the long-term success of your team, the storming stage can appear very counterproductive to where you want your team to be. This stage can be characterized by conflict, fighting, dislike, resistance to your leadership, player isolation, and general hostility, and defensiveness. This is a time when you might see your team begin dividing and splitting into opposing groups with team members becoming frustrated with one another, the emerging team leadership (captains), as well as any number of coaching decisions. This is also a time when competition among teammates escalates, as teammates begin to assert themselves in what they say and how they act. In short, a "storm" generally entails your team being somewhat polarized, with varying degrees of interpersonal conflict. It is a natural progression of all teams . . . so prepare for team storming.[1]

COACH UP Strategies

1. Build your team. When a storm arrives, the *"building leadership style"* is a must.[2] Because this stage is marked by conflict and fighting, it is important for you to be more purposeful in "building up" and supporting your athletes. Since your athletes are no longer getting the needed support from their teammates (because they are fighting with each other) they will likely look to you (their coach) for the support and encouragement they need and desire. Many athletes will continue to have questions about their roles and "fit" on the team . . . so continue telling them what to do . . . but also *"build them up"* with encouraging words, praise, and support. At this point in the season, many athletes are not yet fully competent to perform and not yet sold out (committed) to the outlined goals. In addition, their ability to work together and be productive (as a team) is very low. Be purposeful in praising individual behavior and explaining "why" you are asking for and expecting what you are. When the storms hit, build up and support your athletes.

2. Expect a storm. Expect your athletes to be in conflict and fight . . . at least a little. It's what naturally follows individuals coming together and groups being formed. Storms are normal and should be expected. For many teams, this stage can (and often does) "pass with time" as individuals acknowledge and eventually overcome their differences. The goal is for team members to "rise above" their differences, with the result being a more organized, cooperative, and productive team.

> Storms are normal and should be expected.

3. Promote honest and open team discussions. Assist your athletes in appropriately expressing and "working through" their thoughts, emotions, and feelings . . . and encourage them to do so in a manner that is beneficial to moving the *team* through the current storm. It is important to have honest discussions centered on overcoming individual and team differences, as well as, coming together as a "unified group" to facilitate productive team growth. If handled correctly, a storm can help your team focus and grow closer.

4. Have a plan for dealing with conflict. Obviously, some storms "persist" and you must intervene to facilitate a resolution. It is critical to have a specific plan in place to help your athletes resolve their interpersonal conflicts, disagreements, and unfulfilled expectations. Expect conflict and have a plan for resolving it (see Rule 24 for specific conflict resolution strategies).

"Confrontation simply means meeting the truth head-on."
- Mike Krzyzewski

1 Tuckman, B. (1965). Developmental sequence in small groups. *Psychological Bulletin, 63,* 384-399.

2 Adapted from: Blanchard, K., Carew, D., & Parisi-Carew, E. (2009). *The one minute manager builds high-performing teams (revised and updated)*. William Morrow.

Welcome team *norming*

"I've always believed that if you put in the work, the results will come."

- Michael Jordan

Norming. Having learned to more effectively deal with conflicts in the storming stage, team members can now begin more productive team interactions. Teams experience norming as individuals better define, understand, and accept their own and others' roles. Athletes must continue to focus on the team goals, as well as

> This stage is about forming a *"**collective identity,**"* where the team goals become more important than any one individual goal.

trust one another to consistently perform their outlined roles. This is also the time when athletes develop a more positive response to coaches and team captains. The norming stage is about your team coming together, cooperating, and improving communication. This stage is about forming a *"**collective identity,"*** where the *team goals* become more important than any one individual goal. While this stage is appealing, many teams never progress to this point, usually because they lack the action plan to move past the storms encountered in the previous stage. Work through the storms . . . then welcome team norming.[1]

COACH UP Strategies

1. Encourage your team. The *"encouraging leadership style"* is most important during the *norming* stage of group development.[2] In this stage, your team is moving away from interpersonal conflict (storming) and toward cooperation, improved communication, and greater team trust. As your team begins to establish this initial cohesion, it will be important to support and praise all positive team interactions. At this point in the season, your athletes have likely learned the majority of the skills they will need for the rest of the season. Because athletes are now focused on improving and refining their skills, this is an important time to build confidence. Confidence building starts by offering encouraging words, promoting and modeling effective team communications, and supporting positive team interactions (see Rule 49 for more on building confidence). Encourage athletes to fulfill their roles and look to build the confidence of those athletes lacking a strong self-belief.

2. Revisit team goals. What is it that your team is trying to accomplish? Revisit team mission and vision statements. Be sure to review any and all strategies for achieving the agreed upon team goals, as well as the time-frames for which to accomplish the goals. Remember, motivation starts with a clearly stated intent (see Rule 14). Athletes are more motivated when they know exactly what it is they are striving to accomplish. Revisit team goals and clearly *re-state* the intent.

> What is expected of each individual must be understood as it relates to the larger team purpose.

3. Re-establish individual and team expectations. Each athlete must clearly understand what he or she is expected to do, what the team is expected to do, and how they are going to work together (combine efforts) to accomplish the outlined tasks. What is expected of each individual must be understood as it relates to the larger team purpose. Every individual should feel important and valued in terms of their role in helping the team successfully reach its goals.

4. Trust the process. To some degree, all teams will progress through these stages. Trust the *process* . . . and trust that your team is moving toward a higher level of performance. High performing teams take time to build and develop. Setbacks, mistakes, and conflicts are inevitable but the process of team building is about overcoming the storms and building cohesive and "together" groups.

"It's amazing how much can be accomplished if no one cares about who gets the credit."

- Blanton Collier

1 Tuckman, B. (1965). Developmental sequence in small groups. *Psychological Bulletin, 63,* 384-399.

2 Adapted from: Blanchard, K., Carew, D., & Parisi-Carew, E. (2009). *The one minute manager builds high-performing teams (revised and updated).* William Morrow.

Enjoy your team *performing*

"Good teams become great ones when the members trust each other enough to surrender the ME for the WE."

- Phil Jackson

Performing. The performing stage is marked by strong team cohesion, individual responsibility, and team accountability. At this stage, team members have learned to effectively communicate and become interdependent . . . and team members understand the importance of each person successfully (and consistently) completing his or her role.

> Athletes understand their roles and perform them in a timely manner.

As a result, there is a greater sense of team commitment, as well as a growing sense of maturity that leads to more trust, cooperation, and synergy toward reaching team goals. In short, your team has become efficient and productive. Team members waste little time as they perform and complete the various tasks asked of them. Athletes understand their roles and perform them in a timely manner. If you have successfully navigated the forming, storming, and norming stages . . . you can now enjoy your team performing.[1]

COACH UP Strategies

1. Trust your players to perform. The *"trusting leadership style"* is critical during the *performing* stage of group development.[2] By this stage, you have successfully led your team through the previous three stages (by telling, building, and encouraging), and it is now time to trust your players (i.e., in their roles, decision-making, leadership, and with team outcomes). This trusting leadership style is characterized by *empowerment*. At this point, your athletes should have already developed a close rapport with one another, their individual roles should be clear and understood, and there should be a genuine desire to work together and accomplish the outlined team goals. With that said, it is time to empower your athletes by trusting them to "do the job." Your athletes know what to do, they have the needed skills, they have their teammates' support, and they know how to work together. They have everything they need . . . so ***"get out of the way."*** Empower your athletes to take charge and act independent of you. If you have your team at this stage, they really don't need much from you. What they need most is to know that you truly believe in them to accomplish what is before them. That's empowerment. Trust them to get the job done.

2. Watch for complacency.
As your team begins to *perform* at a high level, watch for signs of overconfidence. Overconfidence usually shows itself in players not preparing as they have in the past. This might be marked by a change in intensity, inattention to details, poor listening, or less time spent in warm-ups, conditioning, or the weight room. Continue to make your expectations clear *and* expect continuous performance improvements from everyone.

> The best way to show that you trust them is to *talk less* and let the team *do more*.

3. Keep the focus. Continue doing what got you to this stage . . . but make a point to do these things better, more efficiently, and with greater focus and effort. And have fun. If you can keep it fun . . . you *will* keep their focus. Enjoy your team performing.

4. Promote "TEAM." Continue to encourage your athletes to "play as a team." The best way to show that you trust them is to *talk less* and let the team *do more.* Let them do what they have learned and practiced. Let them do what you have coached them to do! Move aside and let them work together and play as team.

"We stand alone together."

From the movie *Band of Brothers* - The Men of Easy Company, 506th Parachute Infantry Regiment, 101st Airborne Division

1 Tuckman, B. (1965). Developmental sequence in small groups. *Psychological Bulletin, 63,* 384-399.

2 Adapted from: Blanchard, K., Carew, D., & Parisi-Carew, E. (2009). *The one minute manager builds high-performing teams (revised and updated).* William Morrow.

Conflict is normal . . . really!

"When a team takes ownership, good things happen."
- Pat Summitt

Conflict is inevitable (see Rule 21). Conflict is a part of all relationships, groups, and teams. Conflict can be found in both winning and losing situations, associated with positive or negative actions, and can exist within close or distant relationships. And conflict can occur whether or not an individual has good or bad intentions. At the heart of conflict is *misunderstanding*. Misunderstandings often

> It is not whether or not conflict exists (it does or it will soon) but rather how you go about handling it.

stem from poor communication, miscommunication, or a complete lack of communication. On teams, conflict can surface as players and coaches work through (and confront) differing values, opinions, goals, circumstances, personalities, or expectations. Whatever the cause, conflict must be dealt with in a way that promotes positive growth for you and your team. You may be in conflict with an athlete, another coach, or you may have athletes in conflict with one another (e.g., seniors and first years, starters and non-starters, or captains and teammates). Regardless of who might be involved, you cannot allow team conflict to sabotage your coaching.

With conflict comes the need to find resolution. Whether the conflict is minor (little impact on your team or daily life) or major (very disruptive to you and your team with potential long-term ramifications), there is often a need for swift and appropriate resolution. If not dealt with, minor issues can quickly turn to major issues. Your attitude, timing, and response to conflict are all critical factors to finding resolution. It is not whether or not conflict exists (it does or it will soon) but rather how you go about handling it. Below are several considerations as you develop a plan for dealing with team conflict.

A 5-Step Conflict Resolution Plan

Step 1 - Start with the right attitude. Remember, attitude is everything (see Rule 2). Be sure that you have the right mindset (one that views conflict as an opportunity for positive growth), the individuals involved have an agreed upon time and place to meet (with limited distractions), and everyone involved is well rested and "prepared" to communicate. The goal is to "talk it through" - with the intent of resolving the conflict.

Step 2 - Identify all obstacles. What's at the core of the conflict? What's getting in the way of your team moving forward? What are the barriers to better communication? What's in the way of developing stronger team trust? What's the problem? If you are not sure, ask. As a team, you must identify the obstacles that are leading to the conflict. You have to know the problem before you can formulate a solution. Identifying the obstacles is at the core of successfully resolving conflict, overcoming communication barriers, and restoring team relationships.

> You have to know the problem before you can formulate a solution.

Step 3 - Brainstorm team options. Prepare a list of all possible options for overcoming the obstacles that are preventing your team from reaching its goals. With your team goals in mind, listen to what is discussed and ask how the various options might help improve team trust, commitment, communication, and goal attainment. At this point, it is important to develop a short list of options that most everyone can agree to.

Step 4 - Move forward with the best option. Pick the best available option to resolve the conflict (and prevent further conflict in the future). Based on the outlined obstacles, develop a plan of action. Without "action," it is impossible to move ahead and overcome the obstacles that have led to conflict in the first place. Great ideas are of no use until they are put into action. From your list of brainstormed team options, choose the best option and agree to implement it today.

Step 5 - Act. Put your ideas in motion. All team members must be clear about and agree to individual responsibilities for resolving the conflict. Each person should have specific responsibilities and there should be an established means for holding one another accountable. If the involved parties are not able to work through the steps or need help in the process, seek out a third party to facilitate the conflict resolution plan. Remember, conflict must be dealt with if your team is going to become the productive, high-performing team it is capable of becoming.

COACH UP Strategies

1. Embrace conflict . . . it's a good thing. Working through conflict is not easy but it is necessary. Since conflict is inevitable and you cannot hide from it, accept and embrace it.

> Resolving conflict is not about winning the battle, it's about finding a solution that most team members agree to, feel good about, and can live with.

2. Pick your battles. There are plenty of opportunities for disagreement and conflict. Yet, it is very important to determine which conflicts are worth your time and effort. If you can find a way to deal with your "differences" and not "go to battle" . . . do so. If not, then approach the conflict in the appropriate manner and at the right time. Prepare to resolve the conflict with a win-win mindset. Resolving conflict is not about winning the battle, it's about finding a solution that most team members agree to, feel good about, and can live with.

3. Find the root. What are you (and others) in conflict about? What *is* the cause of the conflict? What's the real issue? Be honest. Remember, conflicts often surface as a result of differing opinions, values, personalities, goals, perspectives, or expectations. Find the root cause before you move to resolve the conflict.

4. Remember the goal. It's easy to lose sight of a goal in the midst of conflict. Be sure to remind and refocus your athletes on the agreed upon team goals that have yet to be achieved (e.g., effective leadership, strong interpersonal relationships, role clarity, efficient practices, honest coach-athlete communication, team cohesion, or consistent performances). Don't forget the goals . . . they will keep your team moving forward and help focus everyone beyond the conflict.

5. Practice empathy. Empathy takes place when you can communicate to another person that you understand his or her point of view. Empathy is all about the person you are speaking with feeling understood. It's about knowing *how* and *why* someone feels as they do. Empathy is when you understand and the other person feels understood. When others experience empathy, they are less likely to become defensive. As defensiveness decreases conflict resolution usually increases.

"The harder the conflict, the more glorious the triumph."

- Thomas Paine

Adjust to a new generation student-athlete

"People don't care how much you know until they know how much you care."

- John Maxwell

Yes, a new generation student-athlete is here! The "digital age" has brought a new kind of student-athlete to your campus, school, gym, camp, practice, workout, and team meeting . . . and this new generation athlete will likely demand a new kind of coaching. This *"new gen"* might be characterized as pampered, distracted, and "busy" . . . but they are also smart. At first glance,

> If you are not meeting their coaching expectations . . . they generally have no problem speaking their minds.

some of your athletes might lack the work ethic, perseverance, and motivation to excel in their respective athletic roles. However, this generation can be incredibly productive, optimistic, and motivated if the right environment is created. No doubt, this new generation athlete is different. From a young age, they have been *entertained* by "reality" television and the ever-changing and interactive advancements in phones, computers, gaming devises, and music. *So, what should you expect? What can you expect? And how do you best relate to, coach, mentor, empower, challenge, and adjust to this new generation student-athlete?*

For starters, be prepared for your athletes to have high expectations for you and your coaching. If you are not meeting their coaching expectations . . . they generally have no problem speaking their minds. As much as you might desire this new generation to "pay their dues" . . . many of your athletes will probably lack the patience and long-term commitment you are looking for. This new gen athlete is often looking for a more collaborative environment in which coaches and athletes work with, learn from, and respect one another. In short, they want teammates and coaches who are willing to motivate, guide, support, and encourage them in carrying out their roles and responsibilities. They want sincerity, honesty, and consistent positive coaching and team interactions.

Coaching this generation starts with a focus on what they "can do," as opposed to what they cannot. This generation is good at multitasking, they are goal oriented, they are generally positive and optimistic, they like working together (if provided the right environment), and of course, they are incredibly "tech smart." With that said, this generation wants a good leader, someone to respectfully challenge them, and *they want to have fun.* So, focus your efforts on teamwork, technology, structure, excitement, and experiential activities that are fun. If you can create the right team climate . . . they will perform!

COACH UP Strategies

1. Make the moment exciting. Find a new and exciting way to say what needs to be said. What you say *is* important but think about *how* to say it in a different and more exciting way. Give feedback that is constructive and purposeful . . . this generation is all about combining purpose, entertainment, excitement, and play.

2. Get to the point. Whether you are coaching X's and O's, telling a story, or showing a video . . . make your point quickly. This generation is about speed . . . everything your athletes do usually gets a "quick" response. The same is expected from you. Be quick to the point, quick to answer questions, and quick to resolve conflicts.

3. Speak the truth. They *will* "speak their minds" and your athletes generally believe and respect others who are up-front in the same way. They may not always like what you have to say . . . but they will respect you. Speak the truth. Say what needs to be said. Be honest.

4. Coach with pictures. Your athletes' world consists of Facebook, Myspace, cell phones, texting, photo sharing, video games, music play lists, movies, and the internet. They Google, Skype, tweet, text, blog, download, upload, post, Snapchat, Instagram, FaceTime, video conference, and design their own forms of communication on their

> Speak the truth. Say what needs to be said. Be honest.

own personalized websites. Their world is made up of pictures . . . so create "pictures" in your coaching. Show and model what you want and expect. Develop good athlete role models, good captains and leaders, and overall good coaching practices that your athletes can **see** every day. *The image you create is more powerful than the words you speak.* Be sure your athletes see it, as well as hear it.

> If they know you believe in them, they will perform for you.

5. Expect them to perform. Walk the line between coaching and mentoring. Coach up, challenge, *and* nurture your athletes. Invest in developing meaningful and purposeful coaching relationships. If you earn their trust, they will work hard. If they know you believe in them, they will perform for you. Expect them to perform at a high level.

6. Be direct but gentle. When athletes hear you say something negative about one of their teammates, they begin to wonder what you might be saying about them. Say what needs to be said but encourage and empower your athletes too. Be direct but also gentle.

7. Organize "team activities" . . . and promote "family." Prioritize spending quality time with your athletes, as well as developing strong teammate relationships. Capitalize on their desires to work together and "hang out" with their friends. Go bowling, organize more cookouts, try some fun teambuilding activities, and invite your team to your home to meet your "other" family.

8. Teach them *how* to behave, *what* to say, and *how* to respond. Many of your athletes just don't know how to act or what to say in some situations . . . or how to respond to failure, mistakes, or conflict. Many athletes have never been taught how to properly work through adversity or had to do so on their own. They have little experience dealing with a variety of situations, problem solving, or "seeing" the consequences of their actions. In some instances, you just cannot expect some athletes to know how to act, how to respond, or how to interpret the consequences of their behaviors. You are _not_ the parent but many of your athletes still need to be taught how to behave, what to say, and how to respond. It's just the way it is.

"There are two ways of exerting one's strength: One is pushing down, the other is pulling up."
- Booker T. Washington

Construct a climate of success

"Successful people make good choices."

- Lou Holtz

hy would your athletes want to come to another practice, sit through another team meeting, watch more film, or give that extra effort needed to finish a drill? What is it about your team environment that promotes togetherness, commitment, and a strong desire to succeed? What does it take to develop an environment that your athletes want to be a part of every day? In short, *what does it*

> In simple terms, creating a climate of success comes down to putting your athletes in the best possible position to succeed.

take to create a climate of success? For starters, consider how you, your staff, and your athletes define success. Success might be determined by wins or losses, by reaching an agreed upon standard or goal, or by simply getting better and improving over time. However defined, creating a ***success climate*** is critical to the attitude and long-term motivation of your athletes, as well as the future success of your team. In simple terms, creating a climate of success comes down to putting your athletes in the best possible position to succeed. Assess your team environment . . . and look to construct a climate of success.

COACH UP Strategies

1. Determine "climate changers," "climate retainers," <u>and</u> "climate destroyers." First, determine your ***climate changers***. Climate changers regularly impact the team climate in a positive way. These athletes have a knack for "stepping up" and "energizing" their teammates when they need it most. They consistently commit to doing "extra" and doing things better than everyone else . . . and they do so with a great attitude. In short, they change the way everyone thinks, plays, and responds. They are positive, influential, and very good at changing team momentum. Second, take note of your ***climate retainers***. These athletes seem to be content with the status quo. They typically do what is asked, but rarely do extra (at least on their own). They are usually good team members but they do *not* go "above and beyond" what is expected. Retainers can be inconsistent from drill to drill and practice to practice . . . but they are "coachable" and often willing to do more . . . if you ask! Finally, isolate your ***climate destroyers***. These athletes seem to always find a way to destroy some aspect of the team. They often complain about, argue with, and resist just about anyone and everyone. They regularly disagree with practice plans, play calling, leadership styles, and decisions about playing time. In short, these athletes are typically "disgruntled" and unhappy. They are negative and in direct opposition to your "positive" climate changers. They *are* the bad apples that *will* wreck your team. Whenever possible, get rid of your climate destroyers.

2. Provide something of value. Know what is of value to your players. Of greatest value to most athletes is playing time. Of course you cannot provide adequate playing time for everyone. However, "value" might be an opportunity to lead a drill or be an honorary captain for an upcoming game, match, meet, or tournament. Providing value might also take the form of recognizing (in front of teammates) and appreciating (one-on-one) specific players for a job well done (see Rule 19). In fact, providing value might simply be a smile, a "thank you," or an encouraging word that enhances an athlete's confidence. Most athletes value practice and competition environments where they feel "cared for" and appreciated by their coaches and teammates. When athletes get something they value, they usually come back for more.

> When athletes get something they value, they usually come back for more.

3. Instill hope. Is your team environment structured and organized in ways that leave your athletes feeling "hopeful"? Do your athletes leave practices more hopeful than when they arrive? Is there hope for more wins? Better team play? How about a hope for self-improvement? Whether winning, improving, or just having fun . . . providing a sense of hope is important. Athletes need to feel as though there is hope for getting better, doing more, and having more success. Take every opportunity to instill hope.

4. Keep everyone in the moment. Always move your team forward! What's done is done. Help your athletes focus in the present and let go of the past and the future. Remind your athletes to be (and play) ***"in the moment."*** The past cannot be changed and the future is not yet known. ***"Right now"*** . . . is most important. Discussing bad calls, complaining about what has gone wrong, and blaming others for mistakes will not "move your team forward." Keep everyone in the moment *and* moving forward.

5. Develop "distinction." Look for ways to be different, unique, *and* distinct. Distinction is what "sets you apart" from other coaches, programs, schools, and opponents. What makes you distinct? What makes your team distinct? People often want to associate with groups and teams that are different and unique. Distinct teams have a strong sense of loyalty, commitment, and pride . . . often leading to success climates that directly and positively impact individual and team performances. Team members that feel distinct, generally work hard to keep it that way.

15 "Team Climate" Questions

Consider the following 15 questions. Answer the questions as you think the majority of your athletes might answer them. How each question is answered should provide insight into the team climate you are creating each day. If you believe most of your athletes would answer "yes" to the following questions . . . you are probably doing a good job developing a ***climate of success***. To test your own views about your team climate, have your athletes respond to the following 15 questions and compare what you think to what they think.

1. Do I get excited about going to practice?
2. Do I get excited about playing for my head coach? Assistant/ position coach?
3. Do I feel like I have the coaching to get better every day?
4. Does my coach consistently "tell me what to do" (how to improve)?
5. Does my coach set a positive tone?
6. Is my coach encouraging and supportive?
7. Is there a clearly communicated standard for me to strive for each day?
8. Is there a well communicated "expectation" for me in everything I do?
9. Is my coach excited (passionate) about coaching?
10. Is my coach organized?
11. Is my coach demanding but fair?
12. Does my coach really know and understand me?
13. Can I trust my coach?
14. Are practices challenging (hard) but also inspiring and fun?
15. Is our team culture about winning and being the BEST we can be?

Overall, is there a "*team climate*" that is positive, challenging, *and* rewarding?

"You never stay the same. You either get better or you get worse."

- Jon Gruden

Hold everyone accountable

"Alone we can do so little; together we can do so much."

- Helen Keller

Holding others accountable is difficult, often uncomfortable, and yet absolutely necessary. If your athletes are going to grow and develop, and your team is going to mature and progress, you will need strong individual *and* team accountability. Accountability is about empowering, encouraging, and pushing others to accomplish a task. Yet, it is a rare person that "enjoys" being held accountable.

> Holding others accountable is about helping others reach their goals and follow-through with what they initially set out to do.

Who wants to be told they need to gain strength, work harder, commit more, improve their attitude, change their response to mistakes, or communicate more effectively? As the coach and leader, it can be difficult to hold your athletes accountable, as the process of holding another person accountable often ends with that person becoming angry, offended, or feeling "singled out."

The process of accountability, however, does not have to be negative. Holding others accountable is about helping others reach their goals and follow-through with what they initially set out to do. In short, accountability is about helping others do what they said they would do. Below are several coach considerations for establishing individual and team accountability.

COACH UP Strategies

1. Talk "roles." For most athletes, accountability starts with understanding their roles. First, a role must be made clear (*role clarity*). Do your athletes understand what is being asked of them? Second, a role must be accepted (*role acceptance*). Do your athletes accept the roles they are being asked to perform? Third, the role must be performed (*role performance*). Are your athletes willing to perform, and follow-through with completing their roles? Fourth, responsibility must be taken for having performed the role (*role responsibility*). Do your athletes take responsibility for what they have or have not performed? Fifth, accountability to the role must be enforced (*role accountability*). Are your athletes willing to be held accountable to performing their roles, and doing so to the agreed upon and expected standards? And sixth, each role must be consistently performed (**role consistency**). Are your athletes willing to "bring it" every day, consistently performing their roles from drill to drill, practice to practice, and week to week? In sum, accountability is about clarifying individual roles and then challenging team members to take responsibility for consistently completing their team roles as expected.

2. Post scores, times, grade sheets, and statistics. Whenever possible, visually display scores, times, grades, or any related statistic that might help communicate how an athlete is doing compared to teammates, a previously set individual goal, or a team standard. For example, position times can be visually displayed after 40 yard test runs or 10 yard agility runs or max weight tests can be recorded and regularly displayed for power clean, bench press, and squat lifts. Depending on the sport, individual athletes might be "skill-graded" (by position) with their grades posted (and ranked) for all teammates to see. You could also post shooting percentages, first pitch strikes, serving aces, offensive possession times, steals, average field position, turnovers, kicking accuracy, batting average, defensive errors, touches, shots on goal, or split times. Whatever the score, time, or stat . . . display it so that all team members can be compared to one another and held accountable to carrying out their individual and team roles.

3. Set agreed upon time frames. Set realistic and agreed upon time frames for completing tasks and accomplishing goals. Your athletes should "see" their scores, times, and grades in relation to a specified and expected time-frame for reaching

> Your athletes should "see" their scores, times, and grades in relation to a specified and expected time-frame for reaching their goals.

their goals. For example, volleyball players that run a mile before every Monday practice (Mile Monday – see Rule 50) should see their times improve over several weeks. Half-way through the volleyball season, these athletes can see how their individual times compare to a *mid-season mile run team goal* that has everyone running the mile in a specified time. The same comparison can be made later in the season as athletes compare their individual mile run times to the *end-of-the-season mile run team goal*. Goals can be great for directing your athletes' efforts, but goals must be specific *and* have clearly established time frames for when each goal is to be completed (see Rule 18 for more on goal attainment).

4. Follow up with a call, text, tweet, email, or question. A quick phone call, text message, tweet, or email can go a long way to holding your players accountable. In the off-season, when many athletes are away from campus, texting can be an efficient means for "checking up" on your athletes and assessing their workouts and training progressions. During preseason, a quick email or text to the entire team can help to reinforce your outlined team and practice goals. During the season, athletes can be pulled aside after practice and asked specific questions with the intent of holding them accountable to improving their commitment, leadership, or attitude. This means following up with your players to let them know you *are* watching and that you expect them to improve every day.

5. Allow "natural consequences." Every behavior has a consequence . . . some good and some not-so-good. As difficult as it is, allow your athletes to experience the natural consequences of their actions. For example, a starting athlete who breaks the team drinking policy will have to experience the pain of not playing, letting his or her teammates down, and suffering an unexpected loss having been absent from the lineup. As long as the consequences are made clear (at the start of the season), let the consequences of "wrong actions" be experienced. It is not easy watching a player serve a penalty, sit out a game, or miss part of a season, but it is often necessary to mold the long-term *"team behavior"* that is desired, expected, and best serves the team in the future. Accountability *is* difficult but it is absolutely critical for developing a well-defined team identity and "team first" mentality.

> It is not easy watching a player serve a penalty, sit out a game, or miss part of a season, but it is often necessary to mold the long-term *"team behavior"* that is desired, expected, and best serves the team in the future.

"The strength of the wolf is the pack."

- Rudyard Kipling

Understand the 20/80 Principle

"Don't let players who create 20% of the results start to believe they deserve 80% of the rewards."

- Pat Riley

Also called the Pareto Principle[1] (named after Italian economist Vilfredo Pareto), the 20/80 Principle states that "a few usually account for the majority." In other words, a small number of individuals are often responsible for a large percentage of the outcome. In coaching terms, the 20/80 Principle might mean:

- 20% of your athletes produce 80% of the team results.
- 20% of your athletes and staff produce 80% of your coaching "headaches."
- 20% of your coaching provides 80% of your job satisfaction.
- 20% of your efforts lead to 80% of your success.
- 20% of your time produces 80% or your results.
- 20% of your athletes take up 80% of your time.
- 20% of your pre-game or mid-game talks produce 80% of the desired impact.
- 20% of your athletes account for 80% of your overall team communication.
- 20% of your athletes emerge to make 80% of the leadership decisions.

Okay, you get the point. This rule is about priorities . . . and where you spend your time and energy to get the best return on your coaching. If you invest in the wrong 20%, you may not get the coaching results you are looking for. However, if you invest in the right 20%, you can maximize your time and energy returns. The main point is this: *many team factors (e.g., effort, time, work, intensity, commitment, communication, and leadership) are not equally distributed. Some athletes and coaches just do more than others.* So, prioritize your coaching practices and optimize the top 20% of your athletes and staff. In the end, effective coaching might come down to *"investing in a few to do the majority."*

COACH UP Strategies

1. Select your top 20% producing athletes. Single out those athletes who have the most talent, best attitude, are most committed, have great passion, and set the example for work ethic, leadership, and taking ownership and responsibility. Remember, these athletes will lead your team toward success . . . and these "few" will end up doing the "majority" in terms of what is ultimately accomplished by your team. In short, your "top 20%" will be your primary team producers.

2. Spend extra "coach time" with your top 20%. Coach smart! Make sure your top 20% get some extra coaching. Spend a little extra time mentoring, leading, influencing, encouraging, and empowering your top 20%. Coach these athletes so that they are better equipped and more prepared to lead your team. If you invest in them, they will provide a greater return for you.

3. Determine what "only you can do." You have a lot of coaching duties . . . but what are the jobs that *only* you can do? Ask yourself the following questions: What is it that I do best? What is it that I need to do? What is it that I have to do? Am I using my time and energy wisely? If you are the *only one* to make the final decision, call the play, determine the final practice schedule, finalize the travel itinerary, or address the media . . . then do so boldly. Focus on these jobs, prioritize them in order of importance, and develop a plan for completing these tasks in a timely manner. In the same way, determine those coaching duties that someone else can do . . . and consider letting someone else help you.

4. Delegate "the other jobs." If someone else can do the task . . . let them . . . especially if you know they can get the job done, and do the job well. Delegate the task so you can "free-up" your own time and energy. Spend time doing what is going to give you the best return on your time. Do those things that are geared toward your strengths and in line with what you do best. The goal is to prioritize your duties and become more efficient in your coaching. Your time is valuable. Do what you have to . . . and delegate the rest.

> Spend time doing what is going to give you the best return on your time.

5. Don't forget about the middle 1/3. On any given day . . . you have about 1/3 of your athletes "checked in" and ready to play. On a good day, these athletes are focused, ready to listen, coachable, and looking to get better. However, you will also have about 1/3 of your athletes who are "checked out." For a host of reasons, these athletes will be lacking focus, motivation, and a general passion to play. In the middle, you will have another 1/3 of your athletes that could go either way in terms of checking in *or* checking out. This middle 1/3 can "make or break" your team and practice climate for that day. The goal is to influence your middle 1/3 to "check in" and give you the focus, motivation, and passion you are asking for. You still need to spend the majority of your time with your top 20% producers, but also be sure to create a success climate (see Rule 26) that propels that middle 1/3 to want to play hard and commit more. When you get the middle 1/3 on board . . . you have the majority "checked in" and focused on improving.

"Don't take donkeys to the Kentucky Derby."

- Pat Summitt

1 The Pareto Principle is named after Italian economist Vilfredo Pareto (1848-1923), who in 1906, observed that 20% of the Italian people owned 80% of Italy's wealth.

Trust building is team building

"In leadership there are no words more important than trust. In any organization, trust must be developed among every member of the team if success is going to be achieved."

- Mike Krzyzewski

Trust is that special bond you have with your athletes where there exists a mutual give and take of honesty, respect, and understanding. Trust building is about developing "relationships" with your athletes that extend far beyond the sport you coach, the sport they play, or the number of games you win or lose. Building team trust involves caring about your athletes, knowing about their lives,

> No doubt, it takes time and energy to build trust, but establishing strong team trust will likely be the most important job you have this season.

and being available to them in times of uncertainty and need. Establishing team trust means taking the time to inquire about family, dating relationships, career aspirations, academic standing, as well as teammate friendships and interpersonal struggles. Trust building is about getting to know your athletes and truly "connecting" with them. No doubt, it takes time and energy to build trust, but establishing strong team trust will likely be the most important job you have this season. The more trust building you do, the more team building you do. Trust building *is* team building.

COACH UP Strategies

1. Talk about the importance of trust building. Talk to your team about the importance of connecting with one another and building strong team trust. Encourage and empower your athletes to take responsibility for developing genuine, authentic relationships with each other. Your athletes need to know they can trust you but they also need to know they can trust one another. Help your athletes understand how building team trust leads to a stronger and more productive team.

2. Bring your BEST every day. Bring your *best coaching* every day. It's easy to trust someone who is prepared, organized, and gives their best each day. Your athletes must know that you will be "ready to go" every day, every practice, every drill, every meeting, and every game, match, or meet. When you bring your best it models and reinforces your expectation that they bring their best. Bringing your "best" each day builds a team climate of trust and respect.

3. Do something nice when they least expect it (and sometimes when they don't deserve it). When your athletes least expect something nice from you . . . do something nice for them. Doing something nice might include cutting a practice short or giving your team an unexpected day off. Doing the unexpected might entail bringing bagels and juice for after an early morning practice or structuring a practice consisting of "fun drills" in which the winners are rewarded with sub sandwiches. Whatever you do, make a point to do it when your athletes least expect it *and* when they most need it. Assess the "pulse" of your team and know when they need a shortened practice, a day off, or a "fun day" to relax and refocus. Doing something nice for your athletes is always welcomed but it is especially rewarding when they least expect it . . . and even better on those rare occasions when they don't deserve it. Sometimes doing something nice is just the right thing to do . . . even when it's not deserved.

4. Engage your players about life outside sport. Know what is going on in your athletes' lives. As stated in Rule 10, take time to know the names of moms, dads, boyfriends, and girlfriends. Care enough to ask about brothers and sisters, roommate situations, or any other important people or events. Ask about school, summer jobs, upcoming graduations, and future careers. In short, ask questions and engage your athletes. If you "invest" in them, they *will* invest in you . . . and each other.

5. Be consistent in your actions, reactions, and how you coach and manage. Few things are more important than being consistent in what you say, how you act, and how you respond to others. Being "predictable" is good. If your athletes know what

> If you "invest" in them, they *will* invest in you . . . and each other.

to expect, how you will respond, and what you are planning to do, they *will* trust you. Your athletes cannot trust what they don't hear and see. When your athletes know how you will act, react, and manage the team, they will quickly grow to trust you. Trust is earned . . . so be consistent in your actions, reactions, and how you coach and manage your team.

"Trust men and they will be true to you; treat them greatly and they will show themselves great."

- Ralph Waldo Emerson

Practice the
START - STOP - CONTINUE
exercise

"If you can't stand the heat, you'd better get out of the kitchen."

Harry S. Truman

Improving from day to day, practice to practice, and game to game is important. However, getting athletes to "buy in" to the process of small, but consistent improvements can be a difficult task. In the same way, it can be difficult to get athletes to honestly assess their strengths (what they are good at) and weaknesses (what they need to improve). Yet, an important part of good coaching

> ... an important part of good coaching is breaking down individual and team skills so that all team members clearly understand what they need to improve, as well as what the team needs to change or do different in the future.

is breaking down individual and team skills so that all team members clearly understand what they need to improve, as well as what the team needs to change or do different in the future. A great way to get your athletes (and your entire team) to slow down, assess what is good, what needs changed, and what needs improved is the **START-STOP-CONTINUE** exercise. This exercise can help you and your athletes assess what is going well (what the team should *continue* to do), what is not going so well (what the team should *stop* doing), and what would help your team grow and improve (what the team should *start* doing). Although this exercise can be used at any time, it is most beneficial when conducted after preseason and then again at the midpoint of the season or toward the end of the regular season.

COACH UP Strategies

Schedule a team meeting in a place where you have access to a white board, chalk board, or a flip chart. Allow for at least 45 minutes to conduct the exercise. Write out the words **START, STOP,** and **CONTINUE** (in green, red, and yellow if possible) on a white board, chalk board, or three large poster board/flip chart sheets of paper. Leave plenty of room to make a "list" under each heading. Start the meeting by informing your athletes that you would like to discuss *and* answer three questions about the current state of the team. The first

question is about what this team is doing well and should ***continue***
to do. The second question is about what this team is not doing so
well and should ***stop*** doing. And the third question is about what this
team should ***start*** doing in order to improve. It is best to begin on a
positive note by starting with the continue list, then move to the stop
list, and finish with the start list. This way you are finishing your team
meeting with "action strategies" for how to improve individual and team
performances.

1. CONTINUE (in yellow). Right now, what is your team doing well?
What are they doing that they should continue to do? Maybe your
team has good intensity at practices. If your team agrees . . . put it
on the list. If the attitude of the team is good, get attitude on the list.
How about team leadership? Is it good enough to make the list? What
about listening well, playing loose, having fun, and playing together as a
unified team? Whatever your team is doing well and agrees they should
continue to do, get these things on the CONTINUE list.

2. STOP (in red). What does your team need to stop doing? Be
honest here. What must your team stop doing if they are going to
improve? Maybe teammates need to stop being "defensive" when team
members try to hold one another accountable. It might be that some
team members need to stop complaining, whining, and making excuses.
It could be (as a team) they need to stop waiting for someone else to
"step up" and make a play. Maybe your team needs to stop playing
tight, worrying about mistakes, or thinking too much. And maybe your
team needs to stop responding to mistakes in negative and destructive
ways. Discuss what your team needs to stop doing . . . and get your
answers on the STOP list.

3. START (in green). Okay, now that you have a good idea of what
your team needs to *continue* to do *and* what your team needs to *stop*
doing . . . what is it your team needs to *start* doing? Be specific. Does

> The goal of this exercise is to facilitate an open and honest discussion that ends with concrete ways to improve team performances.

your team need to try something new? Maybe your team needs to start playing with passion, enthusiasm, purpose, or a sense of urgency. It could be that some teammates need to take more responsibility for getting to practice on time, completing their warm-ups, and being ready to play when practice begins. Maybe your team needs to improve commitment, take more responsibility, make better decisions, hold one another more accountable, or be more supportive and encouraging. Maybe your team needs to start responding to mistakes in more productive ways. In short, whatever your team needs to START doing, get it on the list. Be clear about what needs to start happening and who needs to take the lead on making it happen. You and your athletes should walk away from this exercise with "action strategies" for how to improve your team. The goal of this exercise is to facilitate an open and honest discussion that ends with concrete ways to improve team performances. Everyone should know what needs to happen and who is doing what. Expectations and responsibilities should be clear. No excuses!

"He that is good for making excuses is seldom good for anything else."

- Benjamin Franklin

The Rules of Leadership

Bring your leaders *in*

"You're looking for players whose name on the front of the sweater is more important than the one on the back . . . ."

- Herb Brooks

As your leaders go, your team goes. If your leaders arrive at practice with a bad attitude, it's a good bet that the rest of the team will quickly adopt a similar attitude. In contrast, if your team leaders model passion, intensity, and commitment, it's likely that you will see similar qualities from the rest of the team. Leaders lead. They lead by example, and when this example is positive, they influence teammates in the direction of positive communication, positive team chemistry, and positive team performances. Most athletes need someone to "set the standard" and lead the way. In fact, many athletes would do more, work harder, stay longer, respond better, and play with more intensity if they just had a good example to follow. In simple terms, you need good team leaders.

Some leaders just have a sense for what to do and when to do it. However, most up-and-coming leaders need help in developing their leader skills. They need help understanding what leadership looks like, as well as how, when, and where to lead. In sum, most leaders need to be taught how to effectively lead.

To lead by example, your leaders must be committed, display unwavering confidence and composure, and "show" their teammates and coaches they are worthy of leading. Once a strong leadership example is set, your leaders can then begin exercising their vocal leadership skills to hold their teammates accountable and "enforce" the rules, standards, and expectations set by you and your coaching staff. With that said, you will need a plan for assessing and developing your leaders. Invest the needed time to *bring your leaders in* (select *your* leaders), then *build your leaders up* (train your leaders), then *branch your leaders out* (let your leaders lead).

> In simple terms, you need good team leaders.

Bring your leaders in. When possible, "***bring in***" (select) leaders who already possess important leadership skills. Specifically, look to select athletes who are committed, have a good attitude, deal with adversity in a positive manner, are confident, and make good decisions. In some ways, these athletes already lead by example. However, these leaders still need to better understand their leader influence, as well as be challenged to take on more defined vocal leadership roles in the future.

The best leadership situation would be to have your more talented athletes evolve as your best leaders. For this to happen, you will have to select one or two of your more talented athletes and then mentor them to develop their leadership potential. Remember, your best leaders must first lead by example. They must *walk it* and *team it.*

COACH UP Strategies

1. Teach your leaders to "walk it." Your team leaders must understand that their leadership starts with what they do . . . *not* what they say. They must "walk it" first. A leader by example is one of the hardest workers on the team, intense, composed under pressure, confident in all situations, and a person of strong character and integrity. The strongest leaders are credible because of what they do. They must earn the right to be vocal (talk).
Teammates must see a leader . . .
before they will follow a leader.

2. Expect your leaders to "team it." The best team leaders also develop a "team first" attitude. They put their TEAM before themselves. They clearly understand that if they can help their team be better . . . they too will be better. Leaders who "team it" come to practice looking for ways to help their teammates improve. They are willing to come early and stay late if it means helping a teammate better a skill, learn a play, practice a routine, or refine a role. Great leaders focus on making others, and the entire team, better every day. They understand they must first *walk it* . . . then *team it* in everything they do.

> Teammates must see a leader . . . before they will follow a leader.

"The quality of your team leaders can make or break your season."

- **Kay Yow**

Build your leaders *up*

"Leadership is extremely important. I tell every team that it's the leaders' team. If they do a good job leading, then we're going to have a great year. Regardless of how much I give them, I cannot be in the locker room after practice, before practice, after games, before games. They're going to spend more time with their teammates than they are with me, so teammates have to take care of each other."

- Roy Williams

Build your leaders up. Once selected, your team leaders must be developed. To do so, you must be willing to set aside the necessary time to "*build up*" (train) your leaders. Most young leaders need support and encouragement as they learn *and* refine their leadership skills. If you cannot provide the needed leadership training or you don't feel you have the knowledge or the time to do so, be sure to seek additional help (e.g., books, on-line training programs, or sports

---

> Training good team leaders will be one of the most important things you do for the future development of your program.

leadership consultants). A proven leadership training program is critical to the complete development of your athletes and team. Training good team leaders will be one of the most important things you do for the future development of your program. Remember, as your leaders go your team goes. Bring your leaders in . . . then take the time to build your leaders up.

COACH UP Strategies

1. Encourage your leaders to "talk it." When your leaders are committed, making good decisions, putting the team first, and consistently leading by example (i.e., they *walk it* and *team it*), they have "earned the right" to verbally support, encourage, and "talk" to their teammates. In reality, anyone can offer positive words to teammates but positive and encouraging words from team leaders who are extremely committed, confident, and composed generally have the greatest impact. When hard working leaders encourage, support, and empower their teammates (talk it) . . . it just means more!

2. Ask your leaders to "support it." Your leaders must also be willing to adopt the role of "team spokesperson." A good "support it" leader must understand the mood of the team *and* be willing to talk to coaches on behalf of the team. Good team leaders have to support their teammates and be a positive voice for their team. In addition, leaders must be willing to "take a stand" for their coaches in terms of supporting what their coaches are saying and promoting. It is a difficult task but good team leaders support their teammates *and* coaches.

3. Promote your leaders to "own it." The best leaders take responsibility for their own actions, as well as team outcomes. Responsible leaders "own it" by taking ownership of team meetings, what happens at practices, how their team performs in competitions, and what takes place in various social/team gatherings. Good leaders take responsibility for their team and everything that surrounds their team. In short, they see themselves responsible for how the team is currently performing and how their team prepares for the future.

4. Empower your leaders to "enforce it." Without question, one of the most difficult team leader roles is to enforce an agreed upon team standard and hold teammates accountable for their performances. Nobody likes to be told they lack effort, their attitude is bad, or their interpersonal interactions are bringing the team down. However, team accountability is a must and the best leaders are willing to say what needs to be said . . . regardless of the situation or personnel involved. You need leaders who are willing to accept the challenge of enforcing higher standards and demanding "extra" from teammates, even if it means teammates sometimes getting angry or resentful. While the enforcing role is difficult, leaders who are willing to "enforce it" often propel their teammates toward greater

> You need leaders who are willing to accept the challenge of enforcing higher standards and demanding "extra" from teammates, even if it means teammates sometimes getting angry or resentful.

successes. Empower your team leaders to enforce a higher team standard.

"Having great leadership is a key to success. It's really the leaders' team, because they are the ones whom the rest of the players, especially the freshmen, look up to when setting the standards. Our team will go as far as our leaders are willing to take us."

- Mike Candrea

Branch your leaders *out*

"A leader is one who knows the way, goes the way, and shows the way."

- John Maxwell

Branch your leaders out. Once you bring your leaders in *and* build your leaders up . . . you are ready for your leaders to "***branch out***" (and lead). At this point, it's all about trusting your leaders to lead. If they consistently *walk it* and *team it* (see Rule 31), *talk it, support it, own it,* and *enforce it* (see Rule 32), then it is time

> Encourage your leaders to "take the lead" in different situations, circumstances, and within different groups.

to let your leaders "*apply it*" and "*expand it.*" Let them lead. Give your leaders the "green light" to stand up and do what is needed, say what is needed, and follow-through with what is needed. Encourage your leaders to "take the lead" in different situations, circumstances, and within different groups. Empower, mentor, and continue to challenge them to lead in the present (today at practice) *and* in the future (after practice, over the weekend, during breaks and days off, after the season, after graduation, and in the years to come). *Bring them in, build them up, and branch them out.* Step aside and let your leaders lead.

COACH UP Strategies

1. Instruct your leaders to "apply it." Encourage your leaders to apply their leadership skills in all areas of their lives (i.e., sport, school, work, family, dating relationships, and various social settings). Leaders must begin to apply their leadership in all situations and circumstances. For example, in addition to being good team leaders, your leaders should also strive to lead in the classroom, at a restaurant, on the team bus, in a hotel lobby, and at a party on a Saturday night. They need to lead their teammates, friends, roommates, and classmates. Encourage your leaders to look for new opportunities to lead and to "apply" their leadership skills whenever possible.

2. Challenge your leaders to "expand it." The best leaders continue to grow and improve as leaders. They look to better their leadership for next year, next season, when they move into a starting role, or when they move on after graduation. Leadership lessons learned in sport should be transferred and refined for the next *"season of life."* As good as some leaders might be, challenge them to "expand" their leadership by reading more books, spending time with other good leaders, and studying effective leaders from sport, business, and education. Challenge your leaders to look ahead and envision themselves developing even better leadership skills for the future. Challenge your leaders to expand and get better.

"No man will make a great leader who wants to do it all himself or get all the credit for doing it."

- Andrew Carnegie

Write a Captain Job Description

"You won't win consistently without good team leadership."

- Pat Summitt

Talent is essential but on most days talent is not enough. You also need good team leaders and captains who "buy in" to your ways of coaching and your system of training, who treat their teammates with respect and dignity, and who are willing to hold their teammates accountable. To consistently win, you will need team captains that demand the best from themselves, their teammates, and you. Your captains should set the tone for practice, keep you and your staff informed, and model responsibility, decision-making, and a strong work ethic. You need captains who are willing to lead by example and hold their teammates to that example. In the end, your captains become the glue that bonds your team and keeps the team together through the good *and* bad times.

Good captainship is essential. But how do you go about identifying team captains? How do you know who will make the best captain? And how do you go about making sure the right person becomes captain? Finding good captains is not easy. For starters, you might consider allowing your seniors to be captains. However, being a senior does not guarantee a good captain-leader. Even if one of your seniors turns out to be a good leader, you may end up with another senior who is not. And one bad captain-leader can be detrimental to your team. With that said, you could select the captains yourself. While this is easy and you get who you want . . . you do risk the possibility that your "coach selections" include players that are not respected or trusted by their teammates. Of course, you could also have your players vote for team captains. Although this is how many captains are selected and it *can* work – all too often the selection process becomes a popularity vote based on "who likes who." With this process, the most-liked teammates serve as team captains . . . but these individuals often lack the leader qualities necessary to be good captains. Furthermore, the most liked players generally have a hard time holding their good friends and teammates accountable. In short, a well-liked teammate does not equate to being a good team captain.

> You need captains who are willing to lead by example and hold their teammates to that example.

There is another option for selecting captains! How about having your athletes "apply" for the captain job? That's right. What if you wrote a **captain job description** and asked all interested athletes to *apply* for the job? With this method, the athlete who applies for the captain job would have to be confident that he or she could effectively carry out all the outlined duties and responsibilities *and* believe they had the needed skills and qualifications to do so. You might also have each player on your team "nominate" one teammate who they think could fulfill the captain role (as it is defined and outlined in the job description). With this method, the position, required roles, responsibilities, skills, and all the captain qualifications can be clearly outlined and discussed prior to any nomination process. You (the coach) can clarify what you want from your captains and your athletes can still have a voice in putting teammates' names forward as possible team captains. In the end, you can "interview" your final candidates . . . and select the one or two athletes you feel will make the best captain(s). The goal is to get your best leaders in the captain roles. Writing a captain job description and interviewing your best leaders can help you reach this goal. Below is an example of a captain job description to help you in creating a job description unique to your team needs and in-line with what you expect from your team leaders and captains.

> The goal is to get your best leaders in the captain roles.

CAPTAIN JOB DESCRIPTION
Blue Raider Basketball (2013-2014)

Job Title: *TEAM CAPTAIN*

Start/End Dates: Start of camp (November 2013) – end of season (March 2014)

Reports to: Head Coach (*name here*)

Position Purpose/Summary: Be a strong ***leader by example*** (one of the hardest workers on the team, displaying a high level of commitment, focus, intensity, passion, and effort) and ***strong vocal leader*** with good communication skills (one who will encourage, support, and positively hold all teammates accountable). The primary purpose of the Basketball ***TEAM CAPTAIN*** will be to positively influence teammates on-and-off the court, at all extracurricular school and non-school activities, and in the local community.

Duties and Responsibilities: The ***TEAM CAPTAIN*** will be expected to:
- Be ***on time*** to all team practices and team functions (at least 5-10 minutes early),
- Promote a ***positive attitude*** and ***positive team interactions*** - every day,
- Provide a ***positive role model*** concerning commitment, intensity, confidence, response to mistakes, composure, hustle, and a "team first" focus,
- Help settle team conflicts and ***be willing to confront*** and ***hold teammates accountable*** for their on-and-off court behaviors,
- Work closely with and be the "***point-person***" for the head coach,

- Encourage and support **all** teammates,
- **Lead** the team throughout the season (in good *and* bad times),
- Perform other related team duties (as needed or requested by the coaching staff).

Working Conditions/Environment: The *TEAM CAPTAIN* will be asked to perform his/her roles at all times. This includes situations when the team is not performing well, in the midst of a bad practice, when teammates are struggling to get along, and when coaches and/ or teammates are negative in what they say and how they interact with one another.

Essential Job Functions: The *TEAM CAPTAIN* will be asked to:
- Be the hardest worker on the team (be the most committed),
- Model mental toughness by remaining confident and focused . . . and by responding to individual and team setbacks/mistakes in an appropriate manner,
- Develop strong interpersonal and team relations (friendships),
- Provide energy and passion,
- Compliment and support teammates,
- Challenge teammates to get better and work harder,
- Confront teammates' negative attitudes, complaining, gossip, and lack of effort,
- Refocus teammates when distracted,
- Make good decisions (on-and-off the floor),
- Check in with the head coach.

Abilities and Skills Needed:
- Passion and enthusiasm,
- Energy and hard work,
- Commitment to be the BEST,
- Good verbal and nonverbal communication skills,
- Strong character (good decision-making),

- Confidence and mental toughness,
- Assertiveness (to do what is needed),
- Composure (to remain cool and calm under pressure).

Qualifications Required: A willingness to go "outside your comfort zone" and push your teammates (and yourself) to a higher level of play . . . every day!

Nominations for TEAM CAPTAIN

If you are confident that you can consistently fulfill the duties and responsibilities of **TEAM CAPTAIN** *and* have the desire, skills, and abilities to do so . . . write your name here: ______________________

If you are confident that a teammate can consistently fulfill the duties and responsibilities of **TEAM CAPTAIN** *and* they have the desire, skills, and abilities to do so . . . write your teammate's name(s) here:

____

____

If you had to pick only one person to be **TEAM CAPTAIN** . . . who would you pick? Write that person's name here: ______________________

"On every team, there is a core group that sets the tone for everyone else. If the tone is positive, you have half the battle won. If it is negative, you are beaten before you every walk on the field."

- Chuck Knoll

Manage yourself

"Act as if what you do makes a difference. It does."

- William James

Good coaching entails managing all aspects of your team. This includes managing in the off-season, pre-season, in-season, and post-season. Managing your team is about being ready for every practice, game, match, race, meet, or tournament. It's about overseeing team schedules, practice plans, travel, rest, player personnel, team dynamics, as well as all day-to-day coaching decisions.

> Managing your team also entails managing yourself.

Managing your team also entails managing yourself. Consistently managing yourself will put you in a position to be more prepared, organized, creative, and relaxed in your coaching. In short, managing yourself is a critical first step to more efficient coach leadership and more productive team play. In all your managing roles . . . don't forget to manage yourself.

COACH UP Strategies

Manage yourself. Take time to assess and manage you. Managing "you" requires managing your *time, energy, thinking, expectations, emotions, response to setbacks,* and *sleep.* Make the effort to "***Manage the Essential 7***". . . you'll be glad you did.

1. Time. To start, you have more time than you think. Managing your time is really less about "time" and more about prioritizing what needs to be done first. Rarely will you consistently get everything you want done . . . done! Things come up, situations change, crises strike, and people need you when you least expect it. Think *priorities* . . . what needs done now? What needs done first?

2. Energy. Direct your energy toward those things that will provide you with the biggest return (see Rule 28). Wasting energy on things outside your control . . . ends up doing just that . . . wasting energy. It is important to "***control the controllables***" . . . and let everything else go. Focus your energy on what you can control. You cannot control what others think, say, do, or write about you . . . but you can control your own effort, intensity, focus, words, and actions. You only have so much energy in a day . . . use it wisely!

3. Thinking. Remember, you move in the direction of what you think (see Rule 3). Keep your thinking positive and geared toward what *can* be accomplished, what *will* be reached, and what *is* yet to come. Thinking about the past, what went wrong, or what you don't have . . . is of no use. Think about right now, what's next, and working with what you have. Keep your thoughts positive and moving in the right direction!

4. Expectations. It's fine to expect a lot as long as you match your coaching expectations to the current situation, time of season, and team personnel. You often get what you expect . . . just make sure what you expect is appropriate and realistic.

5. Emotions. Coaching can produce strong emotions. If not properly managed however, emotions can quickly become a "negative force." For example, uncontrolled anger and frustration generally lead to harsh words, a negative coaching demeanor (poor body language), and critical coaching practices. In the end, mismanaged emotions can lead to ineffective coaching and poor leadership. Managing emotions is important for all coaches . . . in all situations. Be prepared to manage your emotions at *all times*.

6. Response to setbacks. How you respond to setbacks, losses, and mistakes will set the tone for how your athletes and staff respond to the same. Negativism, complaining, arguing, and blaming will only direct your team to do the same (see Rule 8). In contrast, a focus on individual and team strengths, overcoming setbacks, and instilling optimism and hope . . . will model for everyone a more productive response to the situation. How you respond will dictate how your team responds!

> How you respond will dictate how your team responds!

7. Sleep. Like many coaches, you probably don't feel like you get enough sleep. Although there is no magic number for hours of sleep needed, it *is* important to determine how much sleep *you* need in order to function at an optimal level. No doubt, too little sleep can impact your mood, energy, and how you handle stress. Similarly, how much you sleep, and the quality of your sleep can impact your ability to think, focus, listen, and communicate. In short, the quality of your sleep can directly impact the quality of your coaching. To be *your* best, you might need 8 hours of sleep each night. Yet, another coach may need only 6 hours per night. Whatever you do, try to be consistent with your sleeping by getting about the same amount of sleep each night. Start managing your sleep by making sleep a priority.

"A leader can't make excuses. There has to be quality in everything you do."

- Michael Jordan

Organize your staff

"The mark of a good leader is loyal followers; leadership is nothing without a following."

- Proverbs 14:28 (The Message)

Whether a head or assistant coach, you must work closely, efficiently, and effectively with the rest of your coaching staff. As the head coach, it is ultimately your responsibility to have every aspect of your coaching staff in order. As an assistant coach, you must be clear about what is expected from you, as well as your primary responsibilities for *serving* your head coach. In every way possible,

> The entire staff must be clear with all roles, responsibilities, expectations, and time-frames for completing tasks.

the job of an assistant coach is to "assist" the head coach. When your coaching staff is efficient and running smoothly, it puts your team in a position to do the same.

COACH UP Strategies

Organize your staff. Getting the right coach to do the right thing at the right time is critical. The entire staff must be clear with all roles, responsibilities, expectations, and time-frames for completing tasks. Of course, all coaching duties must fall in line with the outlined team goals, as well as any agreed upon coaching standards and behaviors (see Rule 43).

1. Review all team and staff goals. What are you trying to accomplish this season? What are your team goals? What are your collective staff coaching goals? What are your individual coaching goals? Be sure to review all team and staff goals.

2. Agree on staff objectives. Clarify what is needed to accomplish the outlined team *and* staff goals. What coaching strategies must be implemented and followed to reach the set goals? What coaching styles are best? What coaching behaviors are best? What coaching philosophies will guide staff decision-making? And what coaching climate is best for accomplishing the outlined goals?

3. Detail roles and responsibilities. Detail all coaching roles and responsibilities. Who is responsible for what? What are the specific coaching roles for each of the assistants? What are the unique head coaching duties? How might roles and responsibilities change as the season progresses? How do the head and assistant coaches' roles and responsibilities complement one another? Who will be doing what . . . when . . . and where?

4. Develop appropriate deadlines. Develop specific deadlines for completing all coaching responsibilities. Be clear with what each coach is to do *and* when they are to have it done. Every coach duty should have a clear deadline for completion. Hold one another accountable for getting things done . . . on time! In the end, the more efficient and organized your staff is . . . the more prepared and productive your team will be.

> In the end, the more efficient and organized your staff is . . . the more prepared and productive your team will be.

"If you always do what you've always done, then you will always get what you've always gotten."

- John Maxwell

Lead your team

"You develop a team to achieve what one person cannot accomplish alone. All of us alone are weaker, by far, than if all of us are together."

- Mike Krzyzewski

Leading your team will entail getting all athletes and coaches moving in the right direction, doing the right things, at the right time, and for the right reasons. It's about getting teammates and coaches to think like, act like, and perform like a team. A well-led team knows *where* they are going, *how* they are getting there, and *who* is responsible for doing what. The best led teams seem to be composed, focused, and very productive.

COACH UP Strategies

Lead your team. The goal is to build high-performing teams (see Rules 20-23). Remember, physical skills alone are not enough to win most games, matches, or meets. Even the most physically gifted teams need strong leadership, effective communication, well defined goals, and responsible and accountable athletes and coaches. To a large degree, the success of your team will depend on your success as a leader. Successful coach-leaders start by communicating a clear team vision, promoting strong team unity, establishing lasting team trust, and remaining optimistic . . . regardless of the situation.

> To a large degree, the success of your team will depend on your success as a leader.

1. Communicate a clear team vision. Take every opportunity to communicate the team vision. The entire team should be clear as to what they are working toward . . . today, tomorrow, and in the weeks to come. Both short and long-term goals should be known and understood. As the season progresses, remind and refocus your athletes on the team vision. Clarify with your athletes what they are doing and how their roles and responsibilities impact reaching all short and long-term team goals.

2. Promote strong team unity. Use terms like "us," "we," and "our team." Promote a collective team identity by consistently referring to everyone as "one." Remind everyone that their actions and behaviors directly impact the team climate and team productivity. Help to develop a team motto or team slogan that promotes a together and united team. For example, "we win and lose together," "together we stand," or "we are one."

3. Establish lasting team trust. Do all you can to establish lasting team trust (see Rule 5 and 29). Promote taking responsibility for all actions, as well as admitting mistakes. Say *"I'm sorry," "My bad," "That one's on me,"* or *"My fault."* Apologize when you make a mistake and ask for help when you need it. Practice humility. There is something about a humble response that is trustworthy. Remember, how you and your athletes respond to mistakes and setbacks will directly impact your team climate of trust, respect, togetherness, and cohesiveness.

> When the team environment turns negative, you have to be positive.

4. Remain optimistic. Optimism *is* contagious! No doubt your team will under-perform and you will lose games, matches, or meets that you should have won. Similarly, you and your staff will make mistakes in player personnel, team preparation, and play calling. In addition, you will have athletes who are negative about their team, their teammates, and your coaching. When the team environment turns negative, you have to be positive. In the midst of negativism, worry, and doubt, your athletes need you to be positive, encouraging, and optimistic. At some point, all athletes need *reminded, refocused, and reenergized . . .* and they need you to lead with optimism and remain positive about what is yet to come. You can dwell on the past or be optimistic about the future. Your athletes need you to remain optimistic.

"Great teamwork is the only way we create the breakthroughs that define our careers."

- Pat Riley

Create meaningful team-leader awards

"You've got to earn it. You can't count on other people to do your job for you."

- Herm Edwards

More times than not, a team is shaped and molded by a select few athletes who perform at high levels (see Rule 28). These athletes usually dictate tempo, intensity, focus, and the overall team climate. One way to encourage athletes to step up and lead their team is to create *team and leader awards* that are presented on a weekly, monthly, or seasonal basis (i.e., preseason, in season, or

> Team-leader awards are meant to acknowledge individual athlete's extraordinary contributions.

postseason). Team-leader awards are meant to acknowledge individual athlete's extraordinary contributions. They should be significant, prestigious, and fun. Below are several examples of team-leader awards that you can modify to best promote the team climate you are striving to create. Be prepared to present an actual award (e.g., a glue bottle, spike nail, battery, presidential seal, t-shirt, pine board, poster etc.) for each team-leader award you create. The award could be a picture, trophy, plaque, certificate, or any "material possession" that best showcases the award and what it stands for. Be creative and have fun!

COACH UP Strategies

The Glue Award. This goes to the athlete who consistently promotes *team togetherness* in how they play, communicate, and interact with their teammates. This player is the *"glue that binds the team together."*
AWARD: An Elmer's glue bottle, can, or stick . . . or a framed picture of a glue bottle or stick - dated and signed by the coaching staff.

The Nail Award. The *"tough as nails"* award goes to the athlete who best displays both mental and physical toughness. This might be the athlete who regularly models confidence and mental toughness or the athlete who seldom complains about injury or pain (or anything else).
AWARD: A 6-inch spike nail with a string and laminated index card attached - dated and signed by the coaching staff.

The Gnat Award. This award goes to the athlete who shows the greatest *persistence* in playing *relentless defense*. This athlete constantly "nags" any opponent they are matched against . . . they are like a persistent and relentless gnat that won't go away.
AWARD: A close-up framed picture of a gnat - dated and signed by the coaching staff . . . you could also put the picture inside a glass jar with a sealed lid (a gnat in a jar).

The Energizer Bunny Award. The energizer award goes to the athlete who "sets the tone" for practices and competitions in terms of *energy, enthusiasm, and passion*. This athlete displays a never-ending energy while staying focused and composed. They go . . . and go . . . and go!
AWARD: A stuffed bunny or a 6-Volt Duracell battery - dated and signed by the coaching staff.

The Shark Award. The shark award goes to the athlete who consistently displays the most aggressive, *offensive attacking style*. This player shows no intimidation and is willing to attack the net, go to the hoop, make a play, take a shot, drive the lane, run the field, sacrifice their body, win the ball, gain the yard, steal the base, make the kill, or finish the job.
AWARD: A close-up framed picture of a Great White shark attacking its prey - dated and signed by the coaching staff.

The Practice Player of the Week Award. This award goes to the athlete who has the best week of practice. This athlete may or may not "start" but he or she "sets the tone" for focus, intensity, hard work, commitment, and attitude for the week. This player is usually your *"role model athlete of the week."*
AWARD: A t-shirt printed with a slogan or quote fitting of the award. All t-shirts should be distributed to and worn only by those athletes who have earned the award throughout the course of the season.

The Presidential (Leader) Award. This award goes to the athlete who consistently displays the best *leadership by example* (great commitment, character, confidence, and composure) and the athlete who displays the best *vocal leadership* (good at verbally supporting and encouraging teammates, as well as holding teammates accountable). You can have one award for the best overall leader or two separate awards for the best leader by example *and* the best vocal leader.
AWARD: A framed "presidential seal," presidential decal, or picture of the President of the United States - dated and signed by the coaching staff.

The Clutch Award. The "clutch award" goes to the athlete who consistently performs well "*under pressure*" and *when it is needed most*. This athlete does not shy away from any competitive situation and often saves his or her best performances for "clutch" moments.
AWARD: A framed picture of a well-known athlete in your sport making a great offensive play or defensive stand - dated and signed by the coaching staff.

The Pine (Bench) Award. This goes to the athlete who consistently comes off the bench and performs his or her role without complaining. This player *embraces the "reserve" role* and does so with a good attitude and with great energy and excitement.
AWARD: A 1x6 pine board (12-18 inches long) inscribed with the player's name, year, and award description.

The Commitment Award. This award goes to the *hardest working athlete on the team*. This athlete not only completes what is required, but he or she also *consistently does extra*. They might come early, stay late, spend extra time in the weight room, play extra wall ball, take extra reps, shoot extra shots, complete extra yardage, run extra miles, do extra core work, participate in extra drills, or watch extra film. They are always doing extra . . . and it shows in their play.

<u>AWARD</u>: A commitment poster . . . complete with a commitment quote -
dated and signed by the coaching staff.

The Oscar (Best Director) Award. "The Oscar goes to" . . . the
athlete most devoted to keeping the team on task and ***directing the
team toward its goals***. The Oscar Award is for that athlete who
sees the vision, keeps the vision, and regularly reminds teammates of
the vision. The Oscar winner is usually very focused on reaching *all*
outlined team goals.

<u>AWARD</u>: A miniature "Oscar Award" (replica) that is labeled BEST
DIRECTOR - dated and signed by the coaching staff.

The Coaches' Choice (MVP) Award. This last award is for that
"***special athlete and person***" who exemplifies what you want your
program to be about. This award goes to the athlete you might choose
(if given the chance) to put on the cover of your school sports program.
This athlete stands for everything you want in a player and teammate.
This award (and athlete) best represents you and your program. Your
Coaches' Choice might also be your ***most valuable player (MVP)***.

<u>AWARD</u>: This one is up to you . . . but make sure this award is special
in that it "captures" your program, your coaching philosophy, and your
team values.

*"Believe me, the reward is not so great without the
struggle."*

- Wilma Rudolph

The Rules of Communication

Make good communication a priority

"Communication works for those who work at it."

- John Powell

At the core of good coaching is good communication. The best coaches are knowledgeable about their sport, competent in terms of coaching their sport, *and* good at communicating what they know. No doubt, the tone with which a message is delivered is important. In many instances, it's *less about what* is being communicated . . . and *more about how* something is communicated.

> Good communication is about sending the correct verbal *and* non-verbal messages . . . and doing so consistently from person to person and situation to situation.

Communication entails active listening to make sense of what is said, choosing the correct words with which to respond, and speaking at the right time, modeled with the right actions and expressions . . . *and* delivering your message with the right tone. Good communication is about sending the correct verbal *and* non-verbal messages . . . and doing so consistently from person to person and situation to situation. Good communication is not easy! Yet, without good communication, most coaches struggle to remain mediocre at best. Good communication skills come with practice, trial and error, and maturity. These skills take time to develop and refine, but your coaching effectiveness depends on you mastering the verbal and non-verbal messages you send. Good communication is critical to everything you do . . . so make good communication a priority.

COACH UP Strategies

1. Make "face-to-face" time. The best communication is face-to-face. Emails, texts, phone calls, tweets, chats, blogs, and posts *can* be effective forms of communication . . . but the best chance for successful communication is face-to-face. This is especially true when you are sharing new information or providing feedback. When possible, avoid electronic communication mediums when posting player feedback, selecting and posting teams, responding to conflicts, or communicating "no" to an athlete. Face-to-face interactions allow you and your athletes to hear tones, hear and see emotions, and monitor facial expressions and body language. Person to person interactions take more time but they are well worth it in the long run. Make time to spend time . . . face to face. There is no better form of communication.

2. Explain your decisions and actions. Most athletes want to understand *why* you do what you do, say what you say, allow what you allow, respond as you respond, and expect what you expect. They just want to know why. For example: Why is a less talented senior getting more court time than a more talented first year athlete? Why does one athlete "get away with" not playing hard when another athlete is reprimanded? Why do some athletes get more one-on-one coaching than others? Why is a "captain" allowed to display poor leadership, demean teammates, and consistently lead with a negative attitude . . . and not be held accountable? Why is one athlete punished for coming late to a practice (or a team meeting) when another athlete is not? And why is one athlete allowed to make multiple mistakes (and still play) when another athlete is taken out immediately following their first mistake? Whatever your reasons . . . just be honest! Your athletes do not need to know everything . . . but they do need to know some things. They may not like what you have to say but they *are* entitled to some answers. In the end, poor coach communication can directly impact athlete-coach trust, player motivation, proper focus, and the overall confidence of your athletes. When you can, explain your decisions and actions.

3. No mixed messages. What you say and what you do must match. Remember, your actions speak louder than your words. If you want your athletes to remain calm, respond with confidence, and control their emotions . . . communicate to them in a calm, confident, and controlled manner. If you want your team to be "on time," make sure

> Your athletes will believe what they see more than what they hear. What you do and say must be the same.

you are on time. And if you tell your athletes to be "creative" and make plays . . . don't take them out of the game for making a mistake. No mixed messages. Your athletes will believe what they see more than what they hear. What you do and say must be the same.

4. Listen with purpose. Listen with a purpose to understand *what* is being said, *how* the person feels, and *why* they feel as they do. When you actively listen *and* understand, you are in position to respond effectively and appropriately. When you do respond . . . get to the point! Do *not* "over-talk." It's easy to talk too much, too long, and too often. Your athletes want to know what you have to say but they also want to move on to the next thing. Say what you have to say and be done. Fewer words *can* lead to better communication.

5. Ask good questions and "see it for yourself." The best communicators ask good questions. Asking questions provides opportunities to clarify what has already been stated and communicates to your athletes and staff that you are actively listening to what they are saying. The more you ask . . . the more you will understand. Also, do whatever you can to observe and experience people and events first-hand. Hearing about something "*through the grapevine*" is quite different than seeing and experiencing it yourself. Whenever possible . . . see, hear, and experience things *first hand* so you can have your own interpretation of what was said and what happened.

"The more we elaborate our means of communication, the less we communicate."

- J.B. Priestley

Judge less

"Communication is a skill that you can learn. It's like riding a bicycle or typing. If you're willing to work at it, you can rapidly improve the quality of every part of your life"

- Brian Tracy

Good communication is difficult to achieve . . . *and* hard to maintain. Many factors impact the communication process and several communication barriers must be overcome in order to establish consistent, positive, and productive coach communication. Good communication is made more difficult because you cannot control how well others listen, how they perceive the information you present

> View differences as potential team strengths.

to them, or when (and how) they respond. One potential communication barrier is judging others. It *is* easy to judge, stereotype, and label your athletes and staff based on what they say, how they speak, act, practice, play, compete, respond to others, dress, walk, interact with teammates, or who they spend time with. When you judge or stereotype you risk the possibility of labeling others to be someone other than who they are. When you label others you filter their actions and words through who you "think" they are, as opposed to who they really are. When a label does *not* fit (and is inaccurate), labeling becomes a barrier to effective coach communication. Be careful how you judge and label your athletes and staff. Improve your communication by judging less.

COACH UP Strategies

1. Put all preconceived ideas and judgments "on the shelf." Be honest about when you are "quick to judge." Look past any preconceived stereotypes you may have and spend time engaging and interacting with your athletes so that you can "see" how they respond in different situations. Assess individual differences and look to use these differences to benefit the team. View differences as potential team strengths.

2. See through their eyes. Put yourself "*in the other person's shoes.*" Try hard to understand your athletes and staff based on their age, skill level, gender, position, personality, years of experience, interactions with others, and all current team dynamics. Take a little extra time to see things through their eyes. Empathy leads to better communication for both the coach *and* the athlete.

". . . Communication does not always occur naturally, even among a tight-knit group of individuals. Communication must be taught and practiced in order to bring everyone together as one."

- Mike Krzyzewski

Be quick to listen and slow to anger

" . . . Everyone should be quick to listen, slow to speak, and slow to become angry."

- James 1:19 (NIV)

Your athletes and staff need to know that you have time for them, are willing to listen to them, and care enough to address their concerns. If they feel "shut-out," they *will* shut you out. When people do not feel cared for, they often (and quickly) lose their motivation and commitment to work hard. Remember, your athletes and staff will "buy in" to *you* (the person) . . . before they embrace any

> Angry and defensive responses almost always lead to poor communication.

of your rules, goals, or expectations (see Rule 4). Find time to listen . . . your people need to be heard more than you think.

While it is important to listen to and address others' concerns, it is also normal to want to defend your position, views, thoughts, ideas, or actions. Let me be clear, it *is* important to stand up for what you believe to be right and know to be true. After all, you *are* the coach and you know what you are doing! However, a "defensive" response can make effective communication nearly impossible. Defensiveness generally results from feeling threatened by your perceptions of what others believe about you - in relation to what you believe about yourself. For example, you believe that you are open and honest in your coach communication. Yet, when you receive written feedback from your athletes and staff, you find that many of them perceive your communication to be somewhat closed, unclear, and untrustworthy. As a result, you feel threatened, as your thoughts about your own coaching effectiveness are now in question. For many coaches, this leads to an angry response that is aimed at *"saving face"* and defending past and current coaching decisions, actions, and words. Angry and defensive responses almost always lead to poor communication. As anger and defensiveness increase, your ability to listen and communicate decrease. Be quick to listen and slow to anger.

COACH UP Strategies

1. Set aside scheduled times for your athletes and staff to voice concerns. This could be in the form of a one-on-one meeting, a small group meeting with your captains and team leaders, a weekly staff meeting, or in a team meeting with the entire team. The goal is to hear your team's concerns, what they are struggling with, and what is NOT working. Voicing concerns is *not* the same as venting, griping, or complaining. In fact, in order to promote "team growth" . . . ask your athletes and staff to provide at least one "solution" for every concern, problem, or issue they present. Listen to individual *and* team concerns . . . then move quickly to address the concerns.

2. Practice "one a day." You cannot be available to everyone . . . all the time. And you cannot possibly listen to everyone who needs to talk. With that said, pick "one athlete a day" to listen and respond to in terms of their needs and concerns. No doubt, some athletes will demand more time and attention than others, so hold them accountable to making their points, providing their suggested solutions, and moving on to dealing with the problem. Set aside a few minutes before, during, or after practice to listen and respond to one different athlete each day.

3. Always look to improve. Continue to assess how you can improve your own coaching effectiveness. You may have to alter *how* you communicate, *what* you communicate, *when* you communicate, or *how much* you communicate. Listen to your team and "look for truths" in what you hear from others, see from others, or read in your end-of-the-year coach evaluations. Always look to improve your coaching effectiveness.

> Always look to improve your coaching effectiveness.

4. Just say "no" to defensiveness. Approach a person or a situation having already made the choice to put your defensiveness aside. It's hard to do but it's a decision you make before you start a conversation or approach a situation. You *can* choose to actively listen to what is being stated, assess the information for any truths, and even thank the person for being honest . . . all without becoming defensive! Listen . . . and just say no to defensiveness.

"A beautiful thing happens when we start paying attention to each other."

- Steve Maraboli

Replace critical words with constructive coaching

"This is the team. We're trying to go to the moon. If you can't put someone up, please don't put them down."

- NASA motto

Critical coaching usually involves pointing out mistakes and focusing on what an athlete is doing wrong. In most cases, however, your athletes already know their mistakes and do not need to be reminded of them. A critical focus on a mistake is rarely productive for overcoming that mistake. In fact, focusing on mistakes often results in athletes making the same mistake again. Your efforts and time will be

Coaching is not about pointing out mistakes . . . it's about empowering and coaching athletes toward overcoming their mistakes.

better spent telling your athletes what to do right, building on what they have already done well, and helping them to develop new and improved skills and strategies so they don't make the same mistake in the future. Critical coaching generally leads to a breakdown in coach-athlete communication and critical comments often alienate athletes. In the end, criticism leads to decreased confidence, effort, and motivation. Coaching is not about pointing out mistakes . . . it's about empowering and coaching athletes toward overcoming their mistakes. The most productive coaching is constructive coaching.

COACH UP Strategies

1. Remember . . . they already know their mistakes. Your athletes know when they make a mistake. Be careful not to "rub it in." It's hard enough for your athletes to stop thinking about what they did wrong . . . they need your help focusing on what to do right. The human mind likes to focus on the negatives, the doubts, the mistakes, and the wrongs. Your athletes need help to refocus on the positives, what will go right next time, and what they can do better in the future (see Rules 46-47).

2. Practice constructive "sandwich" feedback. Start with a positive statement about your athlete's play, followed by a clear instruction to help him or her do it better next time, followed by a compliment. Two positives "sandwich" what you instruct the athlete

to do better. For example,
*"Great hustle up the floor . . .
now get to your spot with your
arms straight up . . . your defense
looks solid . . . nice job."* This
form of constructive feedback
is empowering and esteeming
. . . and it promotes a focus
on overcoming mistakes and
improving future performances.
Constructive "sandwich" feedback
propels you and your athletes
toward more productive coach-
athlete communication.

> When you make a habit of sharing the positives . . . your athletes are much more likely to listen, persist, and positively respond when you "coach up" their mistakes.

3. Recognize positive play.

Look for and verbalize positive behaviors that you see. Notice and make
a point to say something about an athlete's positive play, speed, intensity,
attitude, work ethic, hustle, body language, leadership, communication,
or any other positive aspect of their practice or training. The goal is
to recognize positive attributes and behaviors . . . and then clearly
communicate these "positives" to your athletes. When you make a habit
of sharing the positives . . . your athletes are much more likely to listen,
persist, and positively respond when you "coach up" their mistakes.

4. Assume nothing.

Do *not* assume what you have communicated
has been heard or understood. Sometimes, despite everyone's best
efforts, communication fails. To make matters worse, when things
are *not* clear, many athletes are hesitant to ask for clarification.
Communicate your expectations clearly, directly, and often . . . and
do so in both words and in writing (see Rules 43-44). Just because
your athletes don't ask doesn't mean they already know . . . or don't
have questions. If you're not sure what your athletes are thinking or if

they are clear about what you are saying and expecting . . . ask them! Assume nothing. It's better to err on the side of asking more questions and repeating yourself.

"Don't dwell on what went wrong. Instead, focus on what to do next. Spend your energies on moving forward toward finding the answer."

- Denis Waitley

Clarify STAFF expectations, behaviors, and conduct

"The second I let down, particularly if I'm perceived as the leader of my team or my company, I give others an opening to let down as well. Why not? If the person out front takes a day off or doesn't play hard, why should anyone else?"

- Michael Jordan

Important to every coaching staff are the "guidelines" by which all coaches will be held accountable. You should have a clear vision for your coaching style, how you and your staff will "*coach*" in different situations, and clear guidelines for all coaching behaviors and conduct. Although coaching responses and actions are dependent upon specific circumstances and the people involved, clear coaching expectations and guidelines are a must. Your coach expectations should be clearly and directly stated, available (in writing) to each coach, and discussed at the start of each year, and then on an as-needed basis throughout the year. In addition, a means for holding yourself and staff members accountable must be discussed and agreed upon. Below are 30 coach expectations to consider as you develop your own *coaching staff guidelines*. Remember, be clear and direct in what you expect from yourself and your staff.

COACH UP Strategies

STAFF EXPECTATIONS

1. Always be a good role model. Your athletes, fans, and the entire community are watching. You are representing your players, program, institution, conference, community, alumni, and family. Be a good model.

2. Expect more from yourself than others expect from you. Set the "standard" for what is expected in your coach role. Set the bar high . . . and expect more from yourself than others expect from you.

3. Have high expectations for other staff members. High expectations for one another will lead to better long-term coach and team performances. Expect every member of your staff to bring their *best* each day.

4. Be on the same page and speaking the same language. All coaches must be consistent in what they say and do. There can be no coaching confusion or contradictions. Athletes should be hearing *and* seeing the same things from every coach on the staff.

5. Manage your time wisely. Work hard but also smart. Working longer does not always equate to better coaching. Use your time wisely. Manage your time and work smart.

> Work hard but also smart. Working longer does not always equate to better coaching.

6. Follow through on everything. If you have been assigned a coaching duty, it *is* important. *Get it done . . . Do it right . . . Do it on time.*

7. Value each other and all roles and responsibilities. Be loyal to one another, your athletes, your program, and your institution. Everybody is important. Always speak highly of each other and the program.

8. Be on time and ready to go. This means 5-10 minutes early for everything!

9. Give your full attention. Provide your undivided attention to athletes at practices, in team meetings, during film sessions, in coach-athlete meetings, and during all competitions. Your athletes are important . . . so treat them as though they are.

10. Practice constructive coaching. Catch your athletes doing things right. Start with what is positive and going well, build on these positives, and "help guide" them in overcoming all mistakes and setbacks. Offer constructive ways to improve all athlete and staff interactions.

> Keep confidential what is intended to be confidential.

11. Always set the tone. Whether it's your energy, intensity, focus, professionalism, respect, hard work, confidence, perseverance, communication, commitment, or leadership . . . set the tone for everyone else to follow.

12. Share team information wisely and sparingly. Keep confidential what is intended to be confidential. If you're not sure if you should share something . . . don't.

13. Ask for help if you need it. Know what you don't know and ask for help when you need it. Humility is a good thing. Work with your staff and get help when needed!

14. Demand quality in everything you do and in everything you ask for. If you take the time to do something . . . do it right. If you are asking for something, it must be important . . . so make sure what you are asking for is done correctly too.

15. Hold athletes accountable. Hold athletes accountable to all agreed upon roles, responsibilities, standards, rules, and expectations. Athletes should do what you ask, when you ask it.

16. Only ask athletes to do what is needed. Do not waste time with extra drills, meetings, film sessions, or coach speeches. No *over-coaching*. Make your point . . . do what needs completed . . . and be done.

17. Help finish. Everyone works together to set up, change, take down, and finish the job. Working together improves efficiency and productivity.

18. Be the leader. Your athletes are looking to you . . . to lead them. You *are* the coach. Lead your players . . . they are counting on you.

19. Develop position leaders. Help mold team leaders. Teach, empower, and provide leadership opportunities to specific athletes whenever possible. Encourage selected athletes to lead by example *and* develop good vocal leadership skills.

20. Always control your emotions. Manage your emotions and stay composed at all times. Most things are not as good *or* as bad as they might first appear.

21. Be professional in all interactions. Dress appropriately for the occasion, and act in line with your leadership and coaching roles and responsibilities. Do not tolerate arrogant, negative, pessimistic, or demeaning athlete *or* coach behaviors.

22. Keep your athletes engaged and moving. Always motivate your players with "action," passion, and enthusiasm. Do not waste time. Keep everyone engaged and active. If you want them to be excited . . . you be excited!

23. Turn negative feedback into better coaching. All negative coach evaluations or critical written or verbal feedback can be turned into better coaching. Read, listen, and understand where you have gone wrong . . . then make the needed changes to improve your coaching.

24. Coach proper technique and basic fundamentals every day. Strategy, X's and O's, and planning are important . . . but proper execution of basic skills will always be the foundation for good individual and team play.

25. Give credit following a win and take responsibility after a loss. When something goes wrong, take some blame. When you experience success, give others the credit.

26. Trust the plan. Developing great players and successful teams takes time. Trust your coaching plan and the allotted time frame. Success is a process.

27. Fix the problem. Don't let things go. Resolve the conflict, change the practice plan, alter the game plan, decide on the discipline, make the phone call, send the email, schedule the meeting, or talk to the parent. Whatever needs done . . . get it done. *Fix the problem* so you can move forward and get on with better coaching.

> Whatever needs done
> . . . get it done.

28. Set clear coach-athlete boundaries. Your words and actions are powerful. Know your boundaries and adhere to the boundaries surrounding appropriate coach-athlete relationships.

29. Under-promise and over-deliver. Keep striving toward your outlined coaching goals. Find new ways to get better . . . and make sure you deliver on your promises. Provide more than what is expected. Promise less and deliver more.

30. Work harder, prepare more, recruit better, show more class, and coach smarter than your opponents. Do more and do better than other coaches, schools, and programs. Out-coach and out-class everyone else . . . and have fun doing it!

"Individual glory is insignificant when compared to victory achieved as a team."

— **Dot Richardson**

Clearly communicate ATHLETE and TEAM expectations

"I won't accept anything less than the best a player's capable of doing, and he has the right to expect the best that I can do for him and the team."

- Lou Holtz

Athlete and team expectations should be geared toward what you expect from your athletes personally, socially, emotionally, and physically. It is important that you are clear about what you expect from your athletes at practices and competitions, during team travel, in school, off campus, in the community, over holidays and breaks, and at various social gatherings. Of course,

> Your athlete and team expectations will also be the first step toward clarifying a standard of play for your athletes *and* a standard of excellence for your team.

different situations and people will demand different expectations. However, you should have a "core-set" of athlete and team expectations that are somewhat "universal" in that they apply across all situations and settings. As with your coaching staff guidelines, your *athlete guidelines* should be directly stated, provided (in writing) to each athlete, and regularly discussed at different times throughout the course of the sport season. In terms of accountability, you and your staff (with input from your athletes) should be clear as to the consequences for not following the expectations set forth. Again, be specific with what you want from your athletes and team. Your athlete expectations *will* set the tone for the team climate you are trying to establish each day. Your athlete and team expectations will also be the first step toward clarifying a standard of play for your athletes *and* a standard of excellence for your team. Below are 22 expectations to consider as you go about developing athlete and team guidelines for your program.

COACH UP Strategies

ATHLETE AND TEAM EXPECTATIONS

1. BE ON TIME. This means properly dressed, warmed up, and ready to start at the scheduled time.

2. LISTEN. Stop talking, focus, and listen to what your coaches and team leaders are saying. Respect your coaches by giving them your undivided attention.

3. BRING YOUR BEST EVERY DAY. Come ready to compete . . . in everything you do. Mistakes *will* happen but always play hard and do your best . . . every drill, set, serve, play, pass, catch, pitch, hit, kick, block, swim, dive, jump, run, or lift. Give your teammates a reason to trust you.

4. COMMIT MORE. Commitment is doing extra . . . over and above what is already asked. Do extra in the off-season, pre-season, after practice, on weekends, over breaks, in the weight room, and in the classroom. Out-work and out-prepare your opponents.

5. SERVE YOUR TEAM.
Support, encourage, and help your teammates whenever possible. Root for your teammates while on the bench and always speak positively about your teammates, your coaches, and your team. If you don't have anything nice to say, then don't say anything.

> If you don't have anything nice to say, then don't say anything.

6. TAKE SCHOOL SERIOUSLY. Prioritize your studies and do what it takes to be a "good" student-athlete.

7. DRESS APPROPRIATELY. Look nice and "out-class" your opponents in how you look. This includes how you dress on game day *and* how you look in uniform.

8. TAKE RESPONSIBILITY in *defeat* (ask what you could have done to improve your own and your teams' performance) **and GIVE CREDIT** to your teammates and coaches in *victory*.

9. CREATE A HABIT OF RUNNING. Run from drill to drill, to the bench when substituted out of a game, from the bench when substituted into a game, during timeouts, out from the locker room, back to the locker room, and any other time that "hustle" should be the norm. Look good at everything you do.

10. DEVELOP MENTAL TOUGHNESS. Learn to deal with pressure, develop confidence, and maintain focus. Control your emotions at all times. Do what it takes to be "mentally tough."

11. PLAY with INTENSITY, DETERMINATION, and PASSION. If you show up to play . . . play the right way. Take your role seriously. Do your job. Always play hard and with great intensity, determination, and passion.

12. MODEL CHARACTER and INTEGRITY. Make good decisions in and out of your sport. Do the right thing and do it proudly. If you're not sure if you should do something . . . don't do it.

13. TELL the TRUTH and RESPECT YOUR TEAMMATES. Be honest with your teammates and find something to respect about them. You don't have to be best friends but you do have to respect them and what they contribute to the team.

14. LOOK PEOPLE IN THE EYE and COMMUNICATE DIRECTLY WITH THEM. Practice good eye contact . . . and clearly express yourself when speaking to teammates, coaches, classmates, teachers, professors, friends, roommates, family members, and the media.

15. PLAY THROUGH POOR PERFORMANCES, BAD CALLS, and MISTAKES. Get back to performing your role. Focus on what is important for completing your next job. How you respond to your mistakes will determine your long-term success. Be relentless. Keep moving forward and getting better.

> How you respond to your mistakes will determine your long-term success.

16. ABSOLUTELY NO PESSIMISTIC, NEGATIVE, or DEMEANING ATTITUDES . . . and NO COMPLAINING, or WHINING. Absolutely no slumped shoulders, poor body language, negative facial expressions, or negative comments about yourself or any teammate. NO FINGER POINTING . . . unless you are pointing at a teammate to recognize a great play or performance. To play positive you must be positive. Be a positive influence on your teammates and coaches.

17. PLAY TOGETHER. Work together, communicate, and trust one another. The best teams come together and stay together through the good and not-so-good times. You can do much more together than any one of you can do alone. Stick together!

18. PERSIST. Never give up. It takes time to become a champion and it takes time to build a championship team. Work hard, prepare more, and be patient. Never quit on yourself or your team!

19. SAY "THANK YOU." Thank your coaches, teammates, athletic directors, fans, friends, and family. Thank anyone and everyone who

> Say "thank you" to those who sweep the gym, clean the locker room, drive the bus, open doors, serve you food, drive you to practice, and provide you with clean towels and uniforms.

has anything to do with you playing and competing. Say "thank you" to those who sweep the gym, clean the locker room, drive the bus, open doors, serve you food, drive you to practice, and provide you with clean towels and uniforms. Recognize and appreciate those who make it possible for you play and compete.

20. NO PROFANITY. It serves no good purpose. In most instances, swearing is "classless" and is done with a demeaning tone. Profanity does not add to the content of what is being stated. Say what you need to say without swearing.

21. BE A GOOD ROLE MODEL. In everything you do, remember others are watching. Your coaches, teammates, fans, family, and friends are all watching. Always model the appropriate words and actions.

and finally . . .

22. ALWAYS DISPLAY GOOD SPORTSMANSHIP. Regardless of a win or loss . . . always show good sportsmanship. Respect your opponents and *play with class*. Play right and have fun!

"I just try to be consistent. I try every day to help the team win. It might not always be something that shows up in the box score, but every day you can try to do something to help the team."

- Derek Jeter

The Rules of Mental Toughness

Prepare the *body*

"The most important attribute a player must have is mental toughness."

- Mia Hamm

A *mentally tough* athlete is one who approaches competition with great energy . . . yet remains calm. One who is realistic about the current situation . . . yet remains positive and in control of thoughts and emotions. And one who is aware of what is going on in the immediate sporting environment . . . yet remains focused on only those cues that are relevant to successfully completing

> Teaching athletes to *prepare the body, train the mind,* and *sharpen the focus* is the start to developing mentally tough (confident) athletes and teams.

the task. In sum, mental toughness is about ***preparing the body, training the mind, and sharpening the focus***. Like most performers, many of your athletes will need help in developing and improving their mental toughness. At the core of mental toughness training is the recognition of what is within the athlete's control and what is not. Your athletes will have to learn to control what they can (e.g., breathing, muscle tension, emotions, thoughts, and what they look at and listen to) and let go of everything else (e.g., the weather and playing conditions, officiating, opponents' words and actions, what someone thinks, or a play just completed). Teaching athletes to *prepare the body, train the mind*, and *sharpen the focus* is the start to developing mentally tough (confident) athletes and teams. Start with preparing the body.

Prepare the Body. Preparing the body means controlling one's responses to stress and tension. Competitive stress is common and most athletes are all-to-familiar with what happens to their body when faced with performing under pressure or when someone is watching and evaluating their performance. In these performance situations, athletes must ***"prepare to perform"*** as they experience changes in breathing patterns, heart rate, and muscle tension. Preparing the body is about controlled breathing, coordinated muscle movements, and optimal body tension. When not prepared, performance stressors cause muscle tightness, increased awareness to breathing, loss of needed oxygen, and a decreased ability to move in a smooth and "fluid" manner. Preparing the body is about getting ready to perform . . . without stress and tension.

COACH UP Strategies

1. Teach your athletes to "breathe down low." Normal (relaxed breathing) comes from the stomach and when relaxed, the lower stomach rises and falls with every breath. Most relaxed athletes have no problem breathing and rarely think about breathing or how often they breathe. However, when stressed, many athletes take shorter (shallow) breaths that come from the chest region (the chest actually expands as the upper body becomes tight and rigid). Preparing the body starts with controlling one's breathing. This means your athletes must become aware of how their breathing changes given different performance situations. The more stressful the situation, the more "chest breathing" you will likely see. It's important to regularly remind your athletes to stop, take a deep breath (forcing air out through the mouth), and transfer their breathing back to their stomach. Remember, stomach breathing is relaxed breathing. Teach your athletes to *breathe down low.*

> Preparing the body starts with controlling one's breathing.

2. Teach your athletes to "tense and relax." With stress and tension come tight muscles and "jerky" muscle movements. More stress usually means tighter muscles. In short, too much stress leads to decreased physical coordination, which ultimately results in decreased performance. Muscle tension is often observed in shoulders being raised higher than normal (shoulders up toward the ears), hands and arms being drawn close to the body, and a "slumping" posture (slight bending at the waist). Whatever the stress signs, your athletes must be taught how to "relax the body" and *decrease stored up muscle tension.*

One effective means to decrease muscle tension is to tense . . . and then relax specific muscle groups. For example, to relax the shoulder and arm muscles, an athlete can simply make a fist with both hands, slightly bend both arms at the elbows, raise their shoulders up toward their ears, and tighten all the muscles in their forearms, biceps, triceps, neck, shoulders, and upper back . . . hold it for 6-8 seconds and then release and relax. What follows is a relaxed feeling that can be experienced quickly, whenever muscle tension is experienced. This same ***tense and relax*** skill set can be used for any muscle group or body part. The more your athletes practice proper breathing and muscle relaxation, the better they become at preparing their body and controlling their response to stress and tension. But remember, preparing the body is only the first step toward developing mental toughness.

". . . Controlling your destination is better than being controlled by it."

- Jack Welch

Train the *mind*

"*Sometimes the biggest problem is in your head. You've got to believe.*"

- Jack Nicklaus

Train the Mind. Training the mind means controlling one's thoughts, images, and emotions. Your athletes must learn to manage the good *and* not-so-good times. Regardless of the situation or outcome, athletes need to consistently manage what they think about and how they think about and respond to various situations. **Athletes move in the direction of what they think.** Your athletes must understand this, as well as how their mind and body work together. Dwelling on a previous mistake or a recently experienced loss simply "sets athletes up" to experience a similar mistake or loss in the immediate future. In contrast, helping athletes think about their strengths, what they are good at, and what they can do to be successful . . . influences them to move in the direction of success. When engaged in *"success thinking,"* athletes tend to move toward success. When engaged in *"mistake thinking,"* athletes tend to move toward making additional mistakes. In short, it's important to help your athletes control their minds and "think right." Remember, most athletes already have a difficult time staying positive and controlling what goes on in their head. They need your help in moving past a mistake or a loss and training their mind toward success thinking.

COACH UP Strategies

> The body will move in the direction of the image created in the mind.

1. Teach "mental practice." In simple terms, mental practice is "practice that takes place in one's mind." Mental practice takes place when an athlete imagines (even feels) and visualizes (sees) a successful performance before actually performing the task. The more an athlete *"mentally practices"* a task, the more the body becomes "programmed" to perform the task when it is time to do so on the field, court, track, etc. It's important for your athletes to mentally "see" themselves performing the required skill correctly. The body will move in the direction of the image created in the mind. With that said, it is important to help your athletes create images and visions that are positive and contain the specific details (i.e., colors, distances, times, smells, sounds, etc.) and outcomes desired (e.g., a successful catch, shot, throw, defensive play, or team win). As the coach, it is also important to encourage daily mental practice by incorporating a few minutes of mental skills training prior to and during practices and scrimmages. Mental skills are like physical skills . . . the more they are practiced the more effective they will be.

2. Teach your athletes the "5 P's." Your athletes *will* need help in developing positive approaches to training and competitions, maintaining positive perspectives throughout the duration of performances, and responding appropriately following both positive and negative outcomes. *Training the mind* is about helping your athletes control what they think, envision, and feel. To start, most athletes are far more negative than positive. Athletes often think more about what they cannot do than what they can. They also think more about their weaknesses than their strengths and what could go wrong more than what will go right. Given the negative mindset of many athletes, it is important to teach your athletes the **5 P's**. Teach your athletes to move in a positive direction and engage in "success thinking" by helping them establish: 1) a ***positive purpose*** for what they are being asked to do, 2) ***positive expectations*** for what they want (and you want) in their performance, 3) ***positive thoughts*** surrounding their performance and the skills needed to successfully accomplish the desired outcome, 4) ***positive talk*** before and during a performance (i.e., in how they talk to themselves, how they talk to their teammates, and what they hear in return from their teammates and coaches) and, 5) ***positive attitudes*** associated with practicing, playing, and competing. Even when the desired outcome is not reached, your athletes must be encouraged to stay positive, learn from their mistakes, and re-commit to developing

> *Training the mind* is about helping your athletes control what they think, envision, and feel.

their 5 P's. Don't forget . . . training the mind is just the second step in developing mental toughness. In the third and final step, your athletes must learn to *sharpen the focus*.

"Competitive toughness is an acquired skill, not an inherited gift."

- Chris Evert

Sharpen the *focus*

"*Success doesn't come to you . . . you go get it.*"

- Marva Collins

Sharpen the Focus. Sharpening focus means helping your athletes develop and improve their focus on **relevant performance cues**. Your athletes must learn what is *relevant* (when attended to these cues help the athlete perform the task), what is *irrelevant* (when attended to these cues lead to distractions, mistakes, and choking), what is *controllable* (within their control), and what is *uncontrollable* (outside their control). Obviously, focusing on the right cues can be difficult. But focus can be improved. *First*, help your athletes determine the appropriate and ***relevant cues*** given their role on the team *and* the task they are being asked to perform. For a baseball or softball hitter (in the box), the most important cue is the ball. For a basketball free-throw shooter (on the line), a relevant cue might be the front of the rim. And for a linebacker in football, a relevant and appropriate cue might be the eyes of the opposing quarterback as he drops back to make a pass. *Second*, help your athletes determine what is (and is not) within their ***control***. For example, an athlete cannot control the weather or playing conditions, officials' calls, what others think, what the media writes, or the game plan of an opponent. However, athletes can control their own breathing, muscle tension, thoughts, talk, expectations, and what they choose to focus on. Encourage your athletes to "***control the controllables.***" *Third*, develop ***cue words*** to help your athletes get focused, stay focused, and refocus after a mistake. When stated, cue words (or phrases) help athletes mentally and visually focus on the appropriate target. For example, a cue phrase might be "top right" (for the top right corner of a soccer goal), "ball" (to help catch and secure a fly ball), or "zone one" (to prepare for and place a volleyball serve). Whatever the cue, it must be meaningful to the performer and relevant to achieving a successful outcome.

COACH UP Strategies

1. Teach your athletes to "talk out loud." Encourage your athletes to say and repeat (out loud if needed) their various cue words and phrases. For example, a baseball or softball hitter might say "ball" and "quick hands" . . . as they get set in the batter's box. A basketball player might say, "smooth," "easy," and "nothing but net" just prior to shooting a free throw. And a football receiver might say, "ball," "hands," and "up-field" as they prepare to catch a pass and run for the first down marker. The more your athletes "talk out loud" . . . the more they will develop and maintain the appropriate focus needed to perform the task.

2. Teach your athletes to "see big but focus small." To be successful, athletes must be aware of what is going on around them (i.e., without being distracted), and then shift their focus to the one or two relevant cues that will lead to the desired outcome. In short, athletes must be able to *"see big but focus small."* This means they must "see the field" (or court, track, mat, course, pool, or ice) and the position of teammates and opponents, but in order to properly execute a skill or sequence of plays, they must narrowly focus their attention on the smaller details of the task. For example, a basketball point guard must see the entire court but narrowly focus on one teammate to make a successful pass. Similarly, a runner must know and understand his or her lane assignment but only focus on the "start gun" to get the desired start. And a lacrosse player must assess the position of the defense but then quickly focus on the proper angle or yardage to make the appropriate shot on goal. To some degree, many experienced (veteran) players have already learned this skill. However, many of your younger, inexperienced players have not. To help these athletes, be creative in breaking down drills and skills so that players not only understand the need to *"see big"* but also, the importance of *"focusing small."* Seeing big is about starting a performance and focusing small is about finishing the performance and reaching the desired outcome. Help your athletes see big *but* focus small.

> Seeing big is about starting a performance and focusing small is about finishing the performance and reaching the desired outcome.

3. Teach your athletes to "refocus." Following a mistake, a poor performance, or a loss, many athletes will need your help getting refocused. Remember, what's done is done. What's in the past cannot be changed. What's most important is the next trip down the field, up the court, the next shift, at bat, race, shot, serve, possession, offensive play, defensive stand, game, match, or set. Reassure your athletes *("you're okay")* and remind them to control what they can *("control the controllables")*. Then, help them stay in the present *("right here right now")* and focus on the process *("one possession at a time")*. Stay positive and keep it simple. When *you* refocus, *they* will refocus!

"Nothing on earth can stop the man with the right mental attitude from achieving his goal; nothing on earth can help the man with the wrong attitude."

- Thomas Jefferson

Develop personalized performance routines

"Champions don't become champions in the field – they are merely recognized there."

- Bob Costas

Although mental toughness *can* be taught, athletes must develop, practice, and refine these skills in various practice and competitive environments. To do so, it is essential that athletes create ***personalized performance routines***. A performance routine is designed to incorporate unique cue words and phrases that direct the performer to use newly acquired mental skills to ***prepare their***

body, train their mind, and sharpen their focus (see Rules 45-47). A personalized performance routine should be unique to the individual athlete *and* the sport situation. Whatever the routine, it must make sense to the athlete and be regularly used in various practice situations. Once learned, the routine can then be used in competitions. All routines should be developed with the purpose of directing athletes to use the skills necessary to *prepare the body* (breathe and relax muscles), *train the mind* (maintain positive expectations, thoughts, and talk), and *sharpen the focus* (to the relevant and controllable cues).

Different athletes and different sport situations require different "routines." For example, a ***basketball free throw shooter*** might create the following routine:

1. **Settle** – this word might cue the athlete to take a breath and then "tense and relax" specific muscle groups *(to prepare the body),*
2. **Shot** – this might help the athlete to visualize the "perfect shot" *(to train the mind),*
3. **Nothing but net** – these words might help the athlete stay positive, optimistic, and confident *(to train the mind),* and . . .
4. **Front of the rim** – this phrase might help the athlete to focus on a relevant "spot" (based on their shot tendencies) just prior to releasing the ball *(to sharpen the focus).*

A ***pole vaulter*** in track and field might require the following routine:

1. **Ready and back** – this could be a cue to prepare the hands in the proper position on the pole with the right foot back to start (for a right handed vaulter),
2. **Up** – this could be a cue to start the approach with the "pole up,"
3. **Speed** – this could be a cue to increase the approach speed with each running step . . . from step 7-6-5-4-3-2-1,
4. **Plant** – this could be a cue to plant the pole,

5. **Swing** – this could be a cue to swing left with the correct lead leg, and . . .
6. **Finish** – this could be a reminder to finish the vault "strong."

An ***offensive lineman*** in football might practice the following routine:

1. **Feet** – this might help the athlete establish the correct foot spacing and alignment with the other lineman,
2. **Job** – this could be a reminder to quickly "rehearse" what will be required with the snap of the ball,
3. **Count** – this might help the athlete focus on hearing the quarterback's voice (and snap count),
4. **Explode** – this might cue the athlete to "fire off the line" to start a running play or "step back" for the start of a pass play, and . . .
5. **Drive** – this could remind the athlete to "finish" the block and play through the whistle.

A "***generic***" routine that could be applied to any athlete, sport, or situation might be:

1. **Breathe it** – to breathe, then tense and relax the muscles
   (to prepare the body),
2. **See it** – to visualize the proper execution of the required skill
   (to train the mind),
3. **Talk it** – to use the appropriate positive self-talk
   (to train the mind),
4. **Expect it** – to expect a positive performance and outcome
   (to train the mind),
5. **Focus it** – to focus on the relevant performance cues
   (to sharpen the focus), and . . .
6. **Do it** – to "perform" . . . no more thinking
   (just do it).

And one last "***generic***" example:

1. **Relax** – to breathe and relax
   (to prepare the body),
2. **Visualize** – to image and/or visualize
   (to train the mind),
3. **Positive** – to develop positive talk and expectations
   (to train the mind),
4. **Focus** – to focus on the relevant and controllable cues
   (to sharpen the focus), and . . .
5. **Go** – to "do it" . . . finish the task.

> A routine is a "reminder" (to your athletes) to think about, focus on, and execute the skills necessary to prepare the body, train the mind, and sharpen the focus.

Remember, a performance routine will help establish consistent performances. A routine is a "reminder" (to your athletes) to think about, focus on, and execute the skills necessary to prepare the body, train the mind, and sharpen the focus. Consistently implementing and practicing a performance routine will help your athletes develop a greater sense of control, resulting in more confident and focused performances. Performance routines are essential, but your athletes will need guidance in developing a routine that is best suited to their strengths, the situation, and the task expectations.

COACH UP Strategies

1. Understand mental training and how it is important to your sport. Take the time to read about and better understand mental training, as well as how you can positively impact the mental toughness of your athletes. If needed, seek out other coaches or professional consultants who can help you develop a *"plan for mental training."*

2. Take initiative in helping your athletes develop "toughness." Most athletes will need to be taught what it means to be "mentally tough," what skills are required, and how to *prepare the body* (Rule 45), *train the mind* (Rule 46), and *sharpen the focus* (Rule 47). In the end, your athletes will need help creating performance routines that are unique and "make sense" given their sport, position, role, and your coaching expectations.

3. Follow up. Make mental toughness training a normal part of your daily physical practice. Expect your athletes to practice their routines, manage their stress, improve confidence, and remain focused on the relevant and controllable aspects of their performances. Allow time for your athletes to practice their mental skills and performance routines . . . and follow up with them to make sure they are doing what is needed to improve their mental toughness. Talk about it, ask about it, and expect mental toughness every day.

"Sometimes it just takes one player to set the tone and everybody else will follow."

- Sue Bird

Build quiet confidence

"Confidence doesn't come out of nowhere. It's a result of something . . . hours and days and weeks and years of constant work and dedication."

- Roger Staubach

Your coaching credibility is determined by many factors, but none more important than your influence as a "confidence builder." Like it or not, your athletes' confidence is often tied to what they see and hear from you. Your words, actions, and overall demeanor directly impact what your athletes think they can and cannot do, how much they trust themselves to complete a task, and how they respond

> Your words, tone, body language, and facial expressions all influence your players' confidence.

to mistakes and setbacks. Your athletes' confidence is, at least in part, dependent upon your confidence in them. Athletes with confidence are composed, focused, and mentally tough. Confident athletes "play to win." In contrast, athletes lacking confidence often "hold back" and can be easily distracted, anxious, and fearful of making mistakes. Confidence is hard to build, hard to keep, and hard to restore when it is lost. Confidence building can be a delicate process where confidence is "here today" and "gone tomorrow." In fact, it might exist one minute and be gone the next. Confidence (or lack of) might be determined by one bad play, pass, throw, poor shot, false start, missed goal, or dropped ball. Confidence can even be influenced by a facial expression or negative comment from a coach. No doubt, confidence can be fragile and fleeting. However, if approached in the correct manner, you can directly (and positively) impact the confidence of your athletes. Your words, tone, body language, and facial expressions all influence your players' confidence. Don't underestimate your coaching role in developing, maintaining, and restoring your athletes' confidence. Below are 11 considerations for developing confident athletes.

COACH UP Strategies

1. Set them up to succeed . . . especially early on. With success comes confidence. Structure practices to allow for more success to start . . . followed by more difficult skills and drills as the practice progresses. Concerning the team, break down a new offensive or defensive scheme into smaller skill sets and drills that allow for individual player success prior to coming together to practice as a team. Break down skills into easy to manage "steps," creating opportunities to experience success at each step.

2. See the "potential" when they don't. Look beyond where your athletes are now. Look ahead and down the road. Focus on potential. It could be speed, strength, or their ability to see the floor or field. It might be their "coachability" or their desire to learn. It could be their commitment, work ethic, or passion. And it might be their strong character, communication, or leadership. Whatever the potential, *see it and express it.* Talk about what your athletes could be . . . even when they don't yet believe it themselves.

> Talk about what your athletes could be . . . even when they don't yet believe it themselves.

3. Highlight positives and strengths. They may not be doing everything right but find something they are doing well and highlight it as a positive step in the right direction. Recognize and appreciate the right attitude, being in the right position (and at the right time), good hustle, effective communication, proper technique, a good pass, or just a great attempt. Remind your athletes of their power, speed, quickness, or their good leadership. Make sure you take notice and highlight whatever your athletes are doing well today. They may not be doing everything right . . . but they are doing something right. Remind them of their strengths and point out what they already do well.

4. Let them "play through." Allow your athletes time to use and practice their skills, as well as figure out how to overcome their mistakes. When you allow your athletes time to "figure it out" . . . you are showing them you trust them to get the job done. ***Trust from you leads to greater confidence in them***. Athletes that are "pulled" from a game or lineup when they make a mistake often think . . . *"the coach doesn't believe I can do it."* This perceived lack of confidence from you (the coach) can lead to a rapid decline in athlete self-confidence. Give them a chance to *play through* and get it right.

5. Stop swearing and pointing fingers. Harsh words, pointing fingers, angry demeanors, critical words, and swearing almost always have a negative impact on players' confidence. Athletes do not like to be "cursed at." Who does? If swearing and pointing fingers negatively impact confidence . . . then why do it? Swearing can make your point stronger and it might get your athletes' attention . . . but it does little to build confidence. Find something better to say. Your athletes' confidence might depend on it.

> Remind them of the work put in to get to this point in the season or this point in their career.

6. Remind and refocus. Remind your athletes of the time, energy, and commitment they have already put forth toward improvement. The "process" of getting better sometimes gets lost in poor play, a mistake made, a slump, a "funk," or a perceived loss of skill. Remind them of the work put in to get to this point in the season or this point in their career. Also, refocus your athletes on their past successes. Make a *"confidence DVD"* for each athlete that highlights past successes, great plays, and individual positive progress. If a DVD is not cost effective or is too time consuming and difficult to produce . . . make a point to highlight great plays and positive past performances over the course of weekly film sessions or game reviews.

7. Talk about "team confidence." Athlete confidence is often impacted by team play. When teammates play well and with confidence . . . it can impact other athletes to play with confidence. When confident leaders support and encourage teammates, athletes generally respond with more confidence. With that said, when one athlete is struggling with confidence, there should be a strong team presence to help restore and rebuild the lost confidence.

8. Pick your words. Think ahead and have a plan for what you will say to your athletes (see Rule 9). Be ready to respond with *"You can do this," "Come on . . . try again . . . you got this," "You're better than that," "Good job . . . keep going," "Much better,"* or *"Now you're getting it."* Whatever you choose to say, make it sincere, purposeful, positive, and timely.

9. Tell them a story. Do your homework and find a story of another athlete or coach (someone your athletes can relate to) who overcame mistakes, obstacles, or a lack of confidence to reach their goals. The story might even be about you and how you overcame a lack of confidence to become who you are today. It's important that your athletes make the connection that they are not unique or alone in struggling with confidence. It's part of maturing and becoming a better athlete. Everyone has moments in their life where they doubt, worry about, and question if they can do the job. Empower them by letting them know that others have struggled too. Encourage them with a story of someone who overcame a lack of confidence to reach their goals.

10. Understand their perspective. Athletes want to perform well and please their teammates and coaches with good performances. But sometimes they just can't get the job done. They make mistakes because they lack the skill to be successful, they don't yet understand what it is that you expect from them, or they are unable to adequately

> What they need most from you is your support, encouragement, and a reminder that they can overcome their lack of confidence and get past their current struggles.

cope with the pressures associated with their current role. They don't need a coach telling them what they did wrong. They already know. And they don't need a coach yelling or swearing at them for making a mistake. It was not intentional. Remember, most of your athletes already lack self-confidence. What they need most from you is your support, encouragement, and a reminder that they can overcome their lack of confidence and get past their current struggles. They need to know you are there for them and will help them rebuild and restore their confidence. In the most difficult times, they need to know (without question) that you are someone they can turn to and count on as a confidence builder.

11. Celebrate victories and successes. Take time to acknowledge what the team as already accomplished. Verbally recognize and appreciate excellent individual and team play, as well as improvements made and goals attained. Celebrate with time off practice, a restructured practice that includes something different and fun, a barbeque/cookout at your house, or a surprise pizza gathering at a location of your choice. Celebrate for the sake of celebrating, acknowledging successes, and to show your athletes that you appreciate their commitment to you, the team, and the program. Have some fun . . . and make sure your athletes know why you are celebrating.

"Giving people self-confidence is by far the most important thing I can do . . . ."

- Jack Welch

Mold consistent competitors

"Competition is key to developing players. The only practice environment in which you truly develop a player is a competitive arena."

- Anson Dorrance

A true competitor is fun to watch. By all measures, a competitor hates to lose, expects to win, embraces any challenge to improve, and often identifies him/herself by a win or loss. Competitors usually persist and persevere until they reach their goal. And once attained . . . they quickly set a higher standard and then demand even more from themselves and their teammates.

> The goal is to create a *habit* of competitiveness that is expected and promoted every day.

Competitors are also fun to coach. What would it be to have a competitive climate created by the likes of a Tim Tebow, Serena Williams, Derek Jeter, Maya Moore, LeBron James, or Abby Wambach? Imagine that level of competitiveness as a part of your team climate. Not possible? Maybe not . . . unless you have the next Peyton Manning. *But what would it take to develop stronger and more consistent competitors? What would it take to have athletes who are **driven** to pursue "something more," "sold-out" to get better, and truly passionate about winning and being the best?* Obviously, not all athletes can be molded into great competitors. In fact, it is very likely that many of your athletes will never be the competitors you want them to be. In the end, your athletes have to *want* to compete. Still, competitiveness *can* be molded. For many athletes, this means creating practice environments that are more outcome (score) oriented, complete with drills that pit one athlete against another . . . with clear winners and losers. The goal is to create a *habit* of competitiveness that is expected and promoted every day. With competition as the goal, consider a weekly practice schedule that emphasizes individual and team challenges unique to each day of the week.

COACH UP Strategies

1. Mile Monday. How about starting every Monday practice with a timed "mile-run"? Then post each athlete's time for everyone to see and compare. To foster greater competition, post times by age, class, starters and subs, or veterans and rookies (upper class and first year athletes). As the season progresses, post both individual and team improvements.

2. Take down Tuesday. Think about every Tuesday being designated as a "challenge day." On this day, you might end practice by matching-up specific athletes for a "challenge match," where the goal is to "take-down" and beat a teammate (1 v 1). A take-down challenge might correspond with any number of team drills, short scrimmages, or timed matches. The outcome could be based on speed, time, points scored, points allowed, or quality of play. Depending on how it is structured, the challenges could continue until everyone is "taken-down" and there is only one athlete left standing.

3. Warrior Wednesday. A mid-week practice might entail challenging your athletes to go "above and beyond" the normal weekday practice. Consider developing a weekly "warrior award" that is given to that one athlete who displays the greatest commitment by doing more than everyone else. For example, the Wednesday warrior might be the athlete who played with the most passion, had the most intensity, played the best, or did the most extra work for that day. The warrior award could also be a weekly award reserved for that athlete who has had the most consistent and intense practices over the past week. You could even create a warrior award for offense, defense, or a special team of your choice.

4. Thoroughbred Thursday. Thursday might be known as "sprint day." Thursday could become the day where athletes are pitted against one another in speed drills and speed races. Speed challenges can take place in a pool, boat, gym, or on a

> Thursday could become the day where athletes are pitted against one another in speed drills and speed races.

court, field, or track. You can even use a treadmill, stationary bike, or stair-stepper. Be creative here. Develop several speed challenges that your athletes might enjoy . . . and make sure everyone knows the final times, rankings, and winners. . . and then post them until the following Thursday.

5. Final Four Friday. To promote team unity and working together, Fridays might become "team challenge day." Think about dividing your team into smaller, 4-member teams to compete against other 4-member teams. The goal here is to work together in order to accomplish the desired challenge. Team challenges might be judged on quality, efficiency, teamwork, or overall productivity in completing the task. Here, the winning team continues until all remaining teams are defeated. The last team standing becomes the *Final Four Friday Winner.*

6. Super Saturday. Saturday might be "scrimmage day" where one team is crowned champion in a "winner take all" or best of 3 series of scrimmages. Teams might include varsity vs. junior varsity, veteran vs. novice, first team vs. scout team, or any other combination of teams you deem fair and competitive. If Saturday happens to be a regularly scheduled "game day" . . . then Super Saturday can be determined by a *team* win or loss.

> Do something different but still challenge your athletes to "compete."

7. Sunday Fun-day. How about making Sunday . . . a "fun-day" . . . but with a little competition? Sunday might be a day to enjoy a shorter practice with several fun drills and games added. It could also be a day to get away from the normal practice facility to do something different, like go on a trail run or go bowling. It could also be a time for a team barbeque at a coach's house. Do something different but still challenge your athletes to "compete." Challenge individuals to win the drill, cook the best chicken, lead the team on the trail run, have the best average score in bowling, or win the homemade pizza making contest. Have some fun but always keep it competitive.

"Anything where you're keeping score, I want to win."
- Maya Moore

FINAL THOUGHTS . . .

Thank you for reading *Coach Up* and for allowing me to be a small part of your coaching journey. Great coaching does not happen overnight. The best coaches have practiced and refined their skills over many seasons, with many teams, and with countless athletes. Successful coaching is a process that takes much time and energy . . . and demands great patience and perseverance. No doubt, coaching is an art that can be improved from day to day and season to season.

In *Coach Up*, you have been provided **50 Rules** and hundreds of ***"COACH UP Strategies"*** to help you reach your coaching goals. I hope you have been inspired, encouraged, and challenged in your reading. Now it's time to set your sights on being the best coach you can be. It's time to set your coaching bar to a new height. It's time to grow, improve, and expand your coaching. In short, it's time to maximize your coaching talents.

It *is* an honor to be called "coach" . . . and it *is* an every-day challenge to be the teacher, mentor, motivator, team-builder, and leader your athletes want and need. Embrace the power that comes from *Coaching Up*. Somewhere there is an athlete waiting to soar and an ordinary team that is one step away from a championship. Go ahead . . . leave a coaching legacy that your athletes remember for the rest of their lives. Start today. You're already on your way to building more committed, confident, and motivated athletes and teams.

Have fun . . . and always *Coach Up*!

"Excellence is the gradual result of always striving to do better."

- Pat Riley